British Trade Union Posters

BRITISH TRADE UNION POSTERS

An Illustrated History by Rodney Mace

Foreword by Tony Benn

Sutton Publishing

First published in the United Kingdom in 1999 by
Sutton Publishing Limited · Phoenix Mill
Thrupp · Stroud · Gloucestershire · GL5 2BU

British Library Cataloguing in Publication Data
A catalogue record for this book is available from the British Library

ISBN 0 7509 2158 7

Endpapers: 1. 1914. Strike by shop-workers at David Evans, Cardiff.
Frontispiece: 2. 1984. Miners' Strike Support Group stall, Leather Lane Market, London.
Dedication: 3. 1911. National Sailors' and Firemen's Union of Great Britain and Ireland.
Contents page: 4. 1925. Amalgamated Union of Upholsterers members on strike in East London.

 ALAN SUTTON™ and SUTTON™ are the trade marks of Sutton Publishing Limited

Typeset in 9/11 pt Gill Sans.
Typesetting and origination by
Sutton Publishing Limited
Printed in Great Britain by
Amadeus Press Ltd, Huddersfield.

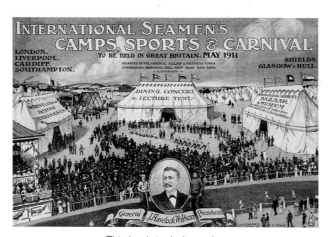

*This book is dedicated to
John Gorman, 1930–1996
printer, socialist and labour historian
whose enthusiasm for posters made this book possible*

Acknowledgements

This book began life in 1988 when John Gorman decided to follow up his very successful *Banner Bright: An Illustrated History of Trade Union Banners* (1973; 1986) with a companion volume on trade union posters. John Gorman was very fitted for this task for he was both a poster printer and labour historian of international standing, so bringing these two passions together in one book was an exciting project. Over the next few years John and I collected, or located the whereabouts of, several hundred posters both in the UK and abroad, but just as we were putting the book together John suffered a fatal heart attack in October 1996. This book is therefore in part his work and I hope reflects well his original intentions of showing how the poster, like the banner, is an important part of the history of the British trade union movement.

This book would not have been possible without the very generous help of John's widow Pamela and their son Jon who have given their unfailing support to the project since the untimely death of a beloved husband and father.

I would also like to thank the following people for their help in making this book:

William Sommerville, The Lipman Trust and The Barry Amiel and Norman Melburn Trust for their financial support.

The staff of the many archives, libraries and trade unions as listed in the source notes at the end of the book.

Phil Dunn and the staff of the National Museum of Labour History.

Christine Coates, Librarian of the Trade Union Congress Collections at the University of North London.

Steve Mills of TUC.

David Shilling of UNISON.

Mary Davis, Richard Ross and Pat Hayes of the Centre for Trade Union Studies, University of North London.

Tony and Caroline Benn.

John Monks and Mike Smith of the TUC who helped convince many unions that the book was a good idea.

Peter Carter, Joe Flemming, Harold Smith, Sid Brown, Paul Martin and Chris Brunel who kindly loaned material from their collections.

To the friends that helped along the way: Ken Sprague, Elizabeth Long, Jane Mace, Jess Mace, Joe Mace, Michael Cunningham, Carlos Sapochnik, Sarah Williams, Roger Thorp, Andrew Reeves, Richard Storey, James Marriott, Ros Lowe, Wayne Seculik, John Tosh.

And to Christopher Feeney and Sarah Moore of Sutton Publishing for their wonderful handling of this book.

Lastly I wish to extend a special thanks to Philip Gell, whose consummate design skills and patience over many months turned hundreds of pictures into a fine book.

Contents

Foreword

by Tony Benn MP

The trade union movement in Britain has never had the same access to the mass media as the rich and powerful. But the posters prepared for demonstrations, strikes and picket lines have always provided a way of getting across the message to those who might not otherwise know what a campaign is all about.

This collection of posters gives a unique insight into the history of the British trade union movement and is a timely reminder of how the struggles and aspirations of working-class people have been important in shaping our society over the last 200 years.

This marvellous book by Rodney Mace, working for many years with John Gorman, should be in every library and on every trade unionist's bookshelf for it gives hope that however difficult the struggle, battles can be fought and won – something the spin doctors and focus groups cannot wish away.

Tony Benn

5. Tony Benn.

Introduction

Since their beginnings 200 years ago trade unions have produced many powerful posters to alert members, communities and the wider world to their struggles for social, economic and political justice. Collected here for the first time are some 200 examples of this output, beginning in 1816 with an appeal by journeymen carpenters against a cut in wages and ending in 1997 with airline workers in dispute over the same issue. On the pages in between are posters that tell of recruitment drives, demonstrations, strikes, meetings and social events held by miners, shipwrights, dockers, tailors, weavers, shop workers, transport workers, printers, health workers and many more of the men and women who have made the history of the British trade union movement.

The posters here have been selected from about 350 uncovered during the research. They are arranged chronologically and grouped into six periods, each period prefaced with its own historical introduction putting the posters in context. At the end of each of these historical introductions are detailed notes on the posters in the section. Almost all of the posters have been dated but where notes are missing altogether or no date has been given, no reliable information on that particular poster is available at present.

The posters are not in themselves a history of trade unionism but more a glimpse of some of the events and moments that have occupied trade unionists from the birth of the movement until today. However, two points are worthy of note: firstly, over the generations, many of the posters have continued to address the same issues – issues that would be familiar to any trade unionist today – for example, the fight for trade union rights and recognition, better pay, safety at work, the need for new recruits, the bad employer, the anti-union government and the importance of public meetings and demonstrations; and secondly that men and men's concerns have long dominated British trade unionism leading to women and their issues being almost absent from posters, despite their being an important part of the movement for more than a century. It has only been in the posters of the last twenty years that women, along with gays, lesbians and black workers, have been portrayed as playing a full part in all aspects of trade union activity.

Needless to say the posters reproduced in this book are but a very small part of all those that have been produced by the movement over the last two centuries. That so many have survived, especially from the early period, is largely down to chance because few trade unions seem to have kept copies of their posters among their records. The posters need to be kept flat and difficulties with both storage and preserving cheap paper on which many were printed meant that after the particular dispute or campaign was over the few remaining posters soon crumbled and were thrown away. Sometimes a branch secretary would think to fold a poster carefully into the back of a minute book but on the whole no file copy was thought worth keeping.

Some early images have survived among the collections of a contemporary who had gathered them together for a particular purpose and whose papers eventually ended up in national or local archives. For example some of the posters relating to the Tyneside shipwrights are from the papers in the British Library of the radical London tailor Francis Place (posters 10–12) who used them in his evidence to the select committees that led to the 1824 and 1825 Combination Acts. In the early 1890s, while writing *The History of Trade Unionism*, Sidney and Beatrice Webb made a collection of posters and handbills which are now in the British Library of Political and Economic Science at the London School of Economics, the institution that they founded in 1895 (posters 41, 58). Local record offices are also a source of both individual posters and in some cases small collections made by antiquarians; examples related to mining in the north-east in the 1840s and '50s are kept at Northumberland Record Office (posters 13–16, 25–32, 34, 35) and images from the campaigns against child labour in the 1830s are found in Rochdale Libraries (20). Beyond these public archives the trade union movement has two major collections of its own – the Trades Union Congress

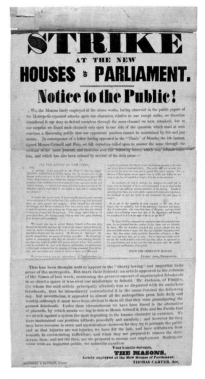

1841. The Operative Stonemasons' Society (see p. 41).

Library and, the richest source of all, the National Museum of Labour History in Manchester – and many posters from both of them are reproduced here. Last and not least among collectors are those individual labour historians whose vigilance and enthusiasm for anything that relates to the history of trade unionism has saved many a poster from the bin.

The role of trade union posters and the language in which they are written has changed markedly over time. Up until about 1860 posters were more like handbills in the way that they advanced arguments and sought to explain and analyse the reasons for a strike or dispute. Some posters, like those of the Tyneside shipwrights in the 1820s (11–15) and the Durham miners in the 1844 (25–32), entered into a public dialogue with other bills put out by employers. A few of the miners' posters also display a common poetic language drawn from English Nonconformity as in Edward Richardson's appeal to fellow workers against the employment of blacklegs (29). Others were inspired by the radical poetry of Shelley and include the men of Seaton Colliery's 'Ye sorrow bitten slaves/Freedom is Life, Slavery is death' (35) and the miners of Haswell and Heaton who cried, 'Union, union! let our watch word be, /And soon the oppressed shall be free . . . Union we must have, or we die' (34). Alongside this poetry there also lies a clear understanding of political economy and the role of labour in the creation of capital as with the 1856 Coventry ribbon weavers' posters (36). Other bills directly address moral questions, for example, the poster about the 1841 masons' strike during the building of the Houses of Parliament where the issue was not wages but that 'the employer not only expected to purchase the labour of a man but also his soul'(33).

From the end of the nineteenth century onwards the messages on posters change from the poetic and rhetorical to the merely declamatory: 'Workmen! Defeat This Attack'(47), 'Great Strike'(49), 'General Manifesto'(52), 'Our Land and How to Get It' (65) and 'Equal Pay for Equal Work' (66). Argument is replaced by moral imperatives which proclaim that the cause being espoused is both just and beyond debate. Nowhere is this more evident than in the extraordinary series produced by the TUC in 1933 and no posters in this book are so clear in their message: 'Socialism = Good Government/ Hitlerism = Gangster Government' (85), 'Socialism – Co-operation – Trade Unionism – Spell Freedom For The Workers' (77) and 'Workless Men – Hoarded Money – Idle Machines – Spell Capitalism' (75).

This change in the form of the posters reflects both the increased self-confidence of the movement and a recognition of the importance of newspaper reports on the progress of industrial disputes. Simply worded posters carried as placards at demonstrations or on picket lines could in themselves become a 'headline' when quoted in a report or reproduced in a news photograph, as can be seen with the 1901 Shop Assistants (61), the 1916 Buxton teachers (66) and most dramatically in the 1933 TUC call for a boycott of German goods (87). A survey of news photographs of trade union actions over the last 100 years shows how important posters have become in getting a union's message across in a clear and unambiguous way. However, the widespread carrying of posters as placards on mass demonstrations, as in the march against the Tories' 1971 Industrial Relation Bill (131), seems to be largely a postwar affair and did not really become a general practice until the 1960s.

After Margaret Thatcher came to power in 1979 posters began to display forceful words like 'Fight', 'Smash' and 'Kick' and images of fists, boots, axes and knives reflected the anger and impatience so many trade unionists felt with the anti-union and free-market philosophies of successive Tory governments (159, 179). In recent years this confrontational style of poster has declined and been replaced by a more gentle image that reflects the more defensive posture trade unions were forced to adopt after eighteen years of Tory anti-trade union legislation, most of which has remained under New Labour. This coupled with a steep decline in membership brought about by de-industrialisation and privatisation has pushed many unions into providing better services for their existing members and into gaining new recruits from some of the burgeoning service industries. A good example of this new mood can be seen in the posters produced by UNISON in the mid-nineties (192, 193).

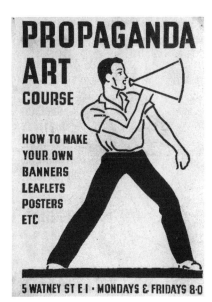

6. 1938. Poster produced for a course on propaganda art made by workers under the direction of Norman King. An exhibition of some of the work was later opened by Herbert Morrison MP.

The way in which posters are manufactured has also been transformed in the last 200 years. Throughout the nineteenth century unions employed local printers who used wood-type to design and make their posters with careful attention being given to simple legibility and eye-catching headlines. Occasionally, as in the Sheffield printers' poster that celebrates the passing of the 1832 Reform Act, elaborate borders and heraldic motifs are used to great effect (18). But it was not until the advent of lithographic printing in the 1890s that posters began to be designed in a modern sense using colour or pictorial illustration. Two examples of this technique are E.J. Kealey's 1911 poster for the International Seamen's Camp, Sports & Carnival (3) and the TUC's 1927 'Tory Attack' poster by Verdilleux (72). Like Verdilleux, the designer Lendon made free use of Soviet-style images in his 1934 Tolpuddle centenary poster but used the bolder colours obtained by hand-made silk screen printing (88). This boldness of colour and design from silk-screen printing was used extensively by some unknown designers employed by National Union of Distributive and Allied Workers and the Union of Shop, Distributive and Allied Workers in the late 1940s and early 1950s (97–101, 104–18) and again in more recent years in many of the posters produced during the 1984 miners' strike (166–9, 171,172).

Over the last thirty years a few unions have employed well-known poster designers like Ken Sprague (149,150), Penny Wild (137), Dan Jones (148), David Kerrigan (153), Dave King (180), Hilary McManus (192,193) and Clifford Harper (189) while others used small sympathetic design companies like the Co-operative Art Service (124), Mountain and Molehill (a small design and printing group that included Ken Sprague and John Gorman) (120–3), Chippenham Posters (147) and Framework (196). Some of the larger unions like the National Union of Public Employees (NUPE) and the National Association of Local Government Officers (UNISON after 1993) have their own in-house design groups which have produced posters to a high standard for more than twenty years including the recent bus-side poster campaign in Scotland (191) and 'the bear' used alongside a recruitment commercial on television (190). Most of the larger trade unions now have publicity departments that employ professional copywriters and designers to get the message of the campaign or event across to both members and a wider world. Although there have been several attempts to help union activists learn how to make better propaganda – most famously in a course put on by Norman King in London in 1938 (6) – it has only been in the last two decades that unions have been sending their members to training sessions on the 'whys and wherefores' of good communications, including how to design better posters. However, there is still an important place for the hand-made, just-for-the-event poster whose pointed wit graces many a demonstration and picket line (7, 178). Very few of these survive the event itself except as recorded in press photographs, although people like Tony and Caroline Benn have made a practice over the years of collecting and taking home a couple from those piles of placards that seem to get left behind after every demonstration.

Lastly, a plea. When the research for this book began ten years ago John Gorman and I expected to find great stores of posters in union offices up and down the country. However, with one or two exceptions, we were to be gravely disappointed; most had been lost or destroyed. The British trade union movement has played an honourable part in the history of this country and will continue to do so but if this involvement is to be better understood by generations to come it is vital that records are safely kept. Perhaps this book will stimulate unions to see more value in their posters as part of that historical record.

7. 1981. A woman worker proudly shows her feelings during a sit-in at Lee Jeans.

The beginnings of trade unionism

In eighteenth-century Britain only very small numbers of the working population were organised into groups to protect themselves and their crafts. Working mostly in towns, groups of skilled artisans like compositors, weavers and boot-makers came together in trade clubs or 'combinations' to protect their rights and privileges, some of which had been guaranteed by Parliament for centuries. For the most part these combinations were seen to be to the benefit of masters and workers alike.

Trade clubs were local social organisations that met in pubs providing (besides beer and good cheer) sickness and burial funds for their members, a place where apprentices were initiated and an address where employers could find workers. Occasionally clubs came together in regional or national unions to petition Parliament to regulate wages or to defend member's rights and privileges against the incursion of non-members into the district. These combinations, along with friendly societies, were to form the roots of the later trade union movement.

For most of the eighteenth century the clubs did not see themselves as radical or political organisations but this was to change markedly during the years of domestic repression which accompanied Britain's long wars with revolutionary France that began in 1793. Influenced by the writings of Tom Paine, republican ideas from America and France and the radicalism of the corresponding societies (organisations of artisans and small tradesmen who campaigned for universal suffrage and annual parliaments), many craftsmen engaged in political struggle and allied themselves with middle-class radicals in the fight for justice and political reform. Fearing widespread conspiracy the state responded by seriously curtailing the activities of any organisation, including combinations, that it saw as a threat to its authority. Three measures affected the combinations directly: the 1797 Act against Illegal Oaths (a response to the naval mutinies of 1797), and the Acts against Combinations of 1799 and 1800.

The 1797 Act struck at the heart of a trade club's activities by singling out as punishable by seven years' transportation the oaths made by new members. The 1799 and 1800 Acts were more directly aimed at combinations themselves for the then Home Secretary, the Duke of Portland, saw them as containing 'within themselves the means of being converted at any time into a most dangerous instrument to disturb the public tranquillity'. But this disguised the Acts' real intent which was to punish workers who had the temerity to combine to raise wages or shorten working hours. The Combination Acts also made strikes and other forms of political activity in the workplace almost impossible. Despite these draconian laws combinations continued to be formed and over the next twenty years resistance, sometimes violent, by workers was met with imprisonment, transportation and even hanging – in the case of the Luddites in 1811–12.

The wars with France were good for employment if not for civil rights; with Wellington's defeat of Napoleon at Waterloo in 1815 the ensuing peace was soon followed by a serious economic downturn and widespread unemployment. The factory system that had flourished under wartime conditions continued to expand, destroying thousands of weavers' jobs and reducing many to a state of penury. In the construction industry the new general contractors were seriously weakening the traditional craft organisations on building sites. Fast-growing towns and factories increased the demand for coal causing mines to be driven deeper and, despite Davy's new safety lamp, conditions and casualty figures among miners worsened significantly. For many workers the postwar period was a time of great hardship as many traditional crafts and ways of life were destroyed by the increasing industrialisation of the workplace. Yet despite the poverty and hopelessness felt by many, political resistance continued only to be met by more government repression, culminating in the Peterloo Massacre at Manchester in August 1819 when eleven people attending an open-air meeting were killed by soldiers.

By 1822 the economy had begun to improve and government opposition to combinations lessened. In 1824 a group of Radical MPs packed a select committee with sympathisers who recommended doing away with the 1799 and 1800 Acts on the grounds that combinations were generally peaceful but not 'very efficient' for they tended to produce 'mutual irritation and mistrust' between worker and employers. Repeal quickly followed but within months opponents to combinations called another select committee whose evidence stated the contrary: combinations were far from the peaceful organisations previously portrayed because they frequently used violence and intimidation against 'non-society men' and in many cases restricted output in order to prevent unemployment. One group of masters in the shipping and shipbuilding industries in the north-east felt particularly aggrieved by such restrictive practices and countered by forming a combination of their own to encourage men not belonging to a union to enter their employ. Within a year similar evidence from around the country pushed a willing government to pass an amending Act which tightened the law on violence, intimidation and obstruction by combinations and narrowed the definition of legal combinations to a matter of wages and conditions. The 1825 Act specifically excluded matters like rules governing the number of apprentices to a journeyman that had survived from previous legislation into the 1824 Act. However the new Act did not stem the tide of workers forming themselves into combinations nor – in a society where only 1 per cent of the population had the vote – did it prevent men from taking direct action to redress their grievances. In 1829 attempts were made to organise the Manchester spinners into a general union to resist wage cuts across the whole industry but this failed as did the London-based, short-lived Grand National Consolidated Trades Union of the early 1830s.

Factories and mines were not only creating a new industrialised working class but they were also generating a new brand of industrialist who was soon clamouring for political power to match his economic strength. Reform of the franchise and the rooting out of the old political corruption, long delayed by war and depression, came to dominate the politics of the late 1820s and many trade unionists allied themselves to the cause of reform in 1830 by joining one of the new pro-reform political unions believing that this would aid their cause. But as the debate intensified it became apparent that a gulf was opening up between the adherents of the new political economy of *laissez-faire* and those who wished to attack capitalism head on. Workers themselves were further divided by the desire of many skilled men to avoid being driven down socially to the ranks of the unskilled or to have their jobs and wages threatened by the child labour that was widespread in the cotton and woollen factories. In the event the 1832 Reform Act only extended the franchise to 7 per cent of the population, and with capitalism and its new masters firmly in place, the state continued to interfere in the affairs of trade unionism.

In 1833, after a Royal Commission had investigated child labour, the government passed a Factory Act which forbade the employment of children under nine years, and limited the employment of those under fourteen to nine hours a day, but many employers avoided the Act by employing children in relays. Women and children had to wait until 1847 for their working day to be limited to ten hours while men had to fight for further twenty-five years to gain similar legislation that would restrict their working day to ten hours.

The agitation for political reform, the fight for shorter hours and the growth of trade unionism left most of the rural population untouched. While the old corruption still dominated the countryside and the landed gentry continued to grow rich, agricultural labourers were suffering greatly from a string of poor harvests that reduced many families to near starvation in the years leading up to 1830. In the eastern and southern counties the situation was particularly bad and, with the introduction of the threshing machine that threatened many a labourer's already meagre winter wages, disturbances seemed inevitable. In November 1830 serious rioting and rick-burning broke out in Kent and quickly spread over the next month as far west as Wiltshire. The government's response was swift: hundreds of labourers were arrested and within a month the Swing Riots were quelled. In January 1831 special courts were set up and after summary justice nearly 500 workers were sentenced to transportation to Australia and many more to hard labour. A few were hanged, including one youth whose only crime was that he had knocked the hat off the head of a member of the Baring banking family.

The savage repression of the Swing Riots failed to suppress rural discontent altogether and a scattering of labourers turned to trade unionism as a means of channelling their continuing grievances against landowners. The government, ever aware of the need to maintain its support in the shires, was not finished with the labourers yet and in early 1834 chose to make an example of six of them from the Dorset village of Tolpuddle who had formed themselves into a friendly society to resist wage cutting. Although none of the men had planned a strike or had attempted to intimidate anyone, they were arrested for conspiracy and sedition under the 1797 Act. The labourers trial, like those of the Swing rioters four years before, was a travesty of justice resulting in the six innocent men, who had only committed a minor offence under common law, being sentenced to seven years' transportation to Australia. The sentences meted out to the 'Tolpuddle Martyrs' caused outrage and did much to consolidate the burgeoning trade union movement of the 1830s. In the event the punishment of the Tolpuddle labourers was remitted in 1836 (23) as was that of many of the transported Swing rioters in 1835.

Ship-Builders

AND

SHIP-WRIGHTS.

THE Journeymen Ship-wrights of the Port of Sunderland, against whom Proceedings have been instituted before the Magistrates for *an illegal Combination to control their Masters,* do hereby acknowledge that they were led to engage in *their late improper Proceedings* under an erroneous Opinion of the Law on the Subject.

Justice-Room, Sunderland, March 19th, 1824.

Sunderland: printed by Reed and Son, 185, High-Street.

8. 1824. Shipwrights' Union Society, Sunderland.

The Posters 1800–1840

The posters in this section embrace three themes that were to dominate the early years of British trade union movement: the struggle to maintain craft skill and wage levels, and to abolish child labour in a time of increasing industrialisation; the use by the State and the employers of anti-trade union legislation; and the fight for political reform.

(9) In 1815 as machines were beginning to replace the traditional hand-block printing of the coarse cotton cloth, calico, employers like the Lancashire company Butterworth, Brooks & Co were using the anti-trade union 1799 and 1801 Combination Acts to oust skilled men and replace them with the much cheaper labour of boys and women.

(10) After many years of depression in the building trade brought on by Britain's long war with France the journeymen carpenters made a public appeal for an improvement in their wages a year after Wellington's defeat of Napoleon at Waterloo in 1815.

(8, 11–16) Fed by a growing coal and iron industry and timber from the Baltic, the north-east shipbuilding industry flourished at the beginning of the nineteenth century and shipwrights jealously guarded their craft organisations particularly in the way apprentices were employed. In an attempt to reduce wages the ship owners used the excuse that the shipwrights were forming an 'illegal combination' to shorten the apprentices' time from seven to three years and that the workers used violence and intimidation against non-union men in contravention of the 1824 Combination Act.

(17) Because domestic hand-loom weaving was being killed off by the new factory system weavers were increasingly under pressure to make agreements with employers in order to safeguard their livelihoods. Besides agreeing wage rates these Rochdale weavers were also promising not to insist on a pre-entry closed shop and to give assurances that the union would give prior notice to the employers of any impending 'turnout' (strike).

(18, 19) Many better-off artisans like the members of the Sheffield Typographical Society celebrated the passing of the 1832 Reform Act in grand style; the Act gave 7 per cent of the population the vote. However,

other, more working-class organisations, such as the Briercliffe and Burnley Political Unions, continued to demand a more radical reform of the franchise. Their demands, along with that of many other democrats, for 'Annual Parliaments, Universal Suffrage, Vote by Ballot and No Property Qualification' were soon to be counted amongst the 'Six Points' that made up the political programme of the Chartism movement during the next generation.

(20) Child labour was essential to the economy of cotton and woollen mills. Tory radicals in Yorkshire organised short-time committees and eventually after a parliamentary campaign a Whig government passed the Factory Act which forbade the employment of children under nine years and limited the working hours of those under fourteen to nine a day.

(21) In the winter of 1833/4 the combined attack of Derby employers on the members of the newly established and short-lived Grand National Consolidated Trade Union led to 15,000 men being locked out. The GNCTU plan – modelled on the ideas of Robert Owen – that members should form cooperatives when on strike floundered through lack of funds and forced the workers back to work.

(22, 23) Despite the fact that trade unions enjoyed some legal recognition through the 1824/5 Combination Acts the government

and judiciary continued to persecute trade unionists with one of the harshest attack being on six farm labourers from the Dorset village of Tolpuddle. In late 1833 in an attempt to resist wage cuts the men formed a friendly society only to be accused three months later of breaking the law by taking illegal oaths: they were sentenced to seven years' transportation to Australia. The 'Tolpuddle Martyrs' case became a cause célèbre and after a concerted campaign by many trade unionists the men's sentences were remitted in 1836.

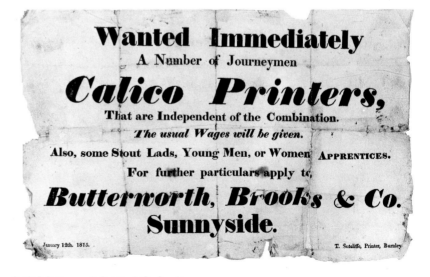

9. 1815. Butterworth, Brooks & Co. Burnley.

The Journeymen Carpenters' VINDICATION

And Expose of the late Meeting of Masters convened to take into consideration the reduction of Journeymens' Wages.

We, the Journeymen Carpenters of London and its Vicinity, being apprised of the intention of those meetings, drew up a Remonstrance against the injustice of such an attempt, conscious that our wages would not admit any reduction under every consideration: our Remonstrance was read from the chair, and breathed that unconfutable argument that admitted no comment. We expostulated on the privations we had endured for the last 4 years, owing to the want of employment ---a great many of us have not had employment more than three-fourths of our time, whereby we have been obliged to pledge the necessaries of life, even our working tools, to procure subsistence for our starving families. Also the depredations committed on our tools and the different expences attached to us by the incumbrances of from 3 to 4 hundred weight on every removal, which, with the wear and loss, must be admitted to reduce our wages not less than **2s.** per week, which makes our wages inferior to that of other mechanics. And now that the bright beams of hope had began to enliven our hearts, and we hailed the blessings of peace as the glad tidings of better times, how great the disappointment when we find the Masters are endeavouring to drive us back into the shades of darkness, and compel us to violate our faith to those who, on the supposition of being able to pay when work became brisk, permitted us to become their debtors. When it was proposed to reduce our wages one-tenth, the principal reason adduced for the necessity of such reduction was, "*their customers had informed them, they should expect the price of labour reduced, or they could not give them any further orders.*" Is it then by reducing the Journeymens' wages that the public will reap such great benefit? We presume the public will judge otherwise; for allowing that **£10** per cent. be taken from the price of labour, the public cannot save more than *Three Pounds Six Shillings and Eightpence per Cent.* from their bills, as there is, on the most moderate calculation, two-thirds for materials.

Perhaps it may be said, the Masters evinced a generous spirit to satisfy their customers--- but, how was it to be done? At the expence of the Workmen! Now, if there were just reasons why the Journeymens' Wages should be lowered, does not the same reasons exist for the reduction of Masters' Profits? This it is manifest they neither do or did intend, which proves them actuated more by self-interested motives than public good.

The Public demanded a reduction in trade, and no other reduction could be admitted by Masters but on Journeymens' labour, notwithstanding Timber, Deals and all other Building Materials have experienced a fall of One-Third! We have not the least doubt had this reduction been candidly stated to the Public, they would have been satisfied without touching the scanty pittance of the Journeymen.

Under these impressions we trust the Public see sufficient reason on our parts to act on such principles as are best calculated to support ourselves and families, however injurious to Masters.

MACDONALD, Printer, 13, Upper Marylebone-Street, Portland-Place.

10. 1816. Journeymen Carpenters of London.

PORT
OF
SUNDERLAND.

Exchange, 8th March, 1824.

At a General Meeting of the Ship-Owners and Ship-Builders, numerously attended, held in consequence of an illegal combination formed amongst certain Ship-Wrights, with a view to compel their Employers into Terms most disadvantageous to the Port,

IT WAS RESOLVED UNANIMOUSLY,—

That the demands made by the Ship-Wrights being illegal in themselves, and if submitted to, of a direct tendency to injure most materially the Shipping Interest, the same should be decidedly rejected.

And that in order to convince such Individuals, that the Ship-Owners and Ship-Builders are not to be intimidated by the threats held out, that they will not return to their employment unless such demands are complied with,

IT WAS ALSO RESOLVED UNANIMOUSLY,—

That the Ship-Builders would not receive back into their employment any of such Ship-Wrights, except on the terms under which they were engaged previous to quitting their employment.

And it also appearing to the Meeting, that certain of the Ship-Wrights have recently formed themselves into a Society, called "The Ship-Wrights' Union Society," ostensibly for charitable purposes, but really to cover improper and unlawful designs,

IT WAS ALSO RESOLVED UNANIMOUSLY,—

That the Ship-Builders would not in future give employment to any Member of that Society. And that to all those Ship-Wrights who withdraw themselves from such said Society and Combination, every encouragement will be given by their Employers, and that protection which the Laws afford, by the Shipping Interest of the Port.

By order of the Societies of Ship-Owners and Ship-Builders of the Port of Sunderland,

JOHN P. KIDSON, SEC.

Sunderland: printed by Reed and Son, 185, High Street.

11. 1824. Society of Ship-Owners & Ship-Builders, Sunderland.

Shipwrights

TO THE

SHIP-OWNERS, &c.

OF THE

PORT OF SUNDERLAND,

GENTLEMEN,

WE, the Shipwrights of the above Port, in answer to a Hand-bill issued by the Ship-Builders, stating, "That our Conduct was illegal, and tended to injure the Shipping Interest," declare such an Assertion to be absolutely false; and, in order to convince the Ship-Owners to the contrary, and that no Intimidation is held out by us, or any Threats used, we are ready and willing to return to our Employment, if the Builders will comply with our just and reasonable Demand.

We most decidedly, and surely not unreasonably, consider a Servant hired for Three Years to be highly injurious to our Trade, and also to the Ship-Owners: and we conceive it to be greatly for the Benefit of this Port and His Majesty's Dock-Yards, that Apprentices should not be taken for a less Term than Seven Years, in order to the upholding of the British Navy.

From the false Mis-representations and calumnious Reports of the Builders to the Ship-Owners, we consider ourselves fully at Liberty, without any fear or dread of a Prosecution by them for an "Illegal Combination," to exercise our Discretion in following our usual Employment for those Owners who may think proper to engage us, and for whom we will exert our utmost Endeavours to give entire Satisfaction.

The Hand-bill alluded to also states, "That *certain* of the Shipwrights have recently formed themselves into a Society, called 'The Shipwrights' Union Society,' ostensibly for charitable Purposes, but really to cover improper and unlawful Designs:" now such an Idea, Gentlemen, we consider can only have arisen from the heated Imagination of some interested Person or Persons, as we feel ourselves perfectly free from the Charge. We would also wish to intimate to the Ship-Owners, that very nearly the whole of the Shipwrights of this Port belong to the above Society; and we conceive the word "certain," as used above, is intended merely to mislead.

Ship-Owners and Ship-Masters may be supplied with Shipwrights for Sea, by applying at Mr. M. Broomfield's, Innkeeper, Bishopwearmouth Panns; or at Mr. R. Todd's, Monkwearmouth Shore.

Sunderland, March 10th, 1824.

12. 1824. Shipwrights' Union Society, Sunderland.

Ship-Builders
AND
SHIP-WRIGHTS.

THE Journeymen Ship-wrights of the Port of Sunderland, against whom Proceedings have been instituted before the Magistrates for *an illegal Combination to control their Masters*, do hereby acknowledge that they were led to engage in *their late improper Proceedings* under an erroneous Opinion of the Law on the Subject.

Justice-Room, Sunderland, March 19th, 1824.

Sunderland : printed by Reed and Son, 185, High-Street.

13. 1824. Shipwrights' Union Society, Sunderland.

AN APPEAL

TO THE

SHIP-OWNERS,

AND THE PUBLIC IN GENERAL.

" Do unto others as you would that others should do unto you."

IT being requested, by a number of the respectable inhabitants of this town, that a true and plain *Statement of Facts* should be distinctly stated, in order to give every person a clear idea of what may be called **OUR GRIEVANCES**, (as many erroneous and unfounded reports have arisen either through ignorance or malice.)

In the first place,—It is said we wish to dictate to our employers; this evidently bears falsehood upon its forehead,—we want no such thing. we wish for nothing more than that a reciprocal interest be established betwixt master and man; for this purpose, reason must be restored to its proper rank—it has been too long degraded—too long neglected—truth is invariable—it is requisite to man—it can never harm him: therefore a few facts will plainly evince our sentiments and requests.

It has been stated to you (the ship-owners) that we would not go to work a-float until we got breakfast; this we deny, and dare challenge any one to come forward to substantiate the assertion.

It has also been intimated to the owners that we would not work unless we had the selection of our own foremen over us; this we publicly and honestly declare to be base in the extreme, and denounce it a lie.

It was also stated by the builders that we were to drop work upon Saturdays, at 4 o'clock, in the afternoon; this is another specimen of detraction, and a thing entirely against the wish of the body of the society; *it was proposed, but was negatived.*

Our real grievances are, that when ordered to work on Sundays, we consider ourselves entitled to double wages for *Sabbath-breaking.*

Again, as a body, we are fully aware that binding apprentices for a less term than 7 years, would be injurious, not only to us, but the builders also, (if they would but see it) and the community at large. Much could be advanced, if necessary, to prove this position: in fact, it would ultimately injure the apprentice himself.

As for regulating wages of any description, either at sea or a-shore, *we deny in toto,* we wish employment, we are willing to do our duty as men, in every sense of the word; and beg leave to add, the sole motive for instituting our fund, is for the good of ourselves and families, being fully confident when that is established, it must, and will in the end, prove beneficial to our employers also. This, gentlemen, is a true statement, which we can substantiate upon oath at any time or place which may be required, and this is what is called *an illegal combination !!!*

South Shields, May 14th, 1824.

MACLIESH AND JOBLING, PRINTERS, COMMERCE STREET.

14. 1824. Shipwrights' Union Society, South Shields.

A COPY

Of the private Rules of a UNION ASSOCIATION of Ship-wrights, whereby the actual nature of the pretensions of that body may be ascertained more accurately than by those Articles which they exhibit to the Magistrates for their approval and enrolment.

PREAMBLE.

When an individual who has a limited power and authority over his fellow-men, attempts to stretch or extend that authority beyond the proper bounds of moderation and justice, it then becomes every one, in whatever situation he is placed, to endeavour to check and suppress that spirit of tyranny and oppression in due time, and before it arrives to any great extent, as it would then be more difficult to accomplish.

Passive obedience and non-resistance are doctrines which do not accord with the feelings of an independent mind; therefore in acknowledging our "pastors and masters," we certainly should not always tamely submit to every thing which they may please to propose, the result of which is to benefit themselves alone. Seeing, therefore, the necessity of establishing a just and lawful equilibrium of right, between the employer and the employed, it becomes the latter, as reasonable men, to stand or pause at every measure likely to be adopted, which bears not alike advantages to master & servant.

In order, therefore, to effect such a laudable purpose, and to remove some of those grievances which have so long existed amongst us, and which have been the bane and ruin of our trade, we have unanimously agreed to establish an Association, to be denominated and called the

UNION SOCIETY,

To be held at the house of Mr. J. Smith, Three Tuns, Old Flesh Market, in the Town and County of Newcastle upon Tyne, subject to the following Rules and Regulations.

ARTICLE I.

That this society shall consist of JOURNEYMEN SHIPWRIGHTS, who have served not less than the space of three years apprenticeship to the business; and to meet every six weeks, between the hours of seven and nine o'clock, at the aforesaid house, where they are to deposit in the hands of the treasurer, or such other officer belonging the society as shall be appointed to receive the same, the sum of *tenpence*, and *twopence* to be spent; and in case of non-payment before the books are closed, each member so neglecting shall be fined *twopence*.

2. All persons desirous of becoming members of this society, shall be admitted *free of entrance money*, for the term of six months from the date of the society; after that period, *five shillings* entrance will be charged, and all arrears then due; at and after the expiration of twelve months *ten shillings* and *sixpence* entrance, and all arrears for the year.

3. Persons entering immediately on the expiration of their apprenticeships, shall have the privilege of becoming free members on paying the sum of *five shillings* entrance.

4. Every member of this society. of two years' standing, on being rendered incapable of following his employment shall receive *two shillings* per week from the fund of this society; independent of a voluntary subscription, to be made by the whole of the members present at the next meeting after the said member shall have declared himself upon the box.

5. That no member shall, during the time of his receiving relief from the society, be called upon for his contribution; but before any relief shall be granted, all fines and arrears must be paid up.

6. When any member dies, his widow, or (if none) his next of kin, shall be entitled to receive the sum of *five pounds* towards defreying the said member's funeral expences. If a member's wife or mother die, *five pounds* shall be allowed as above. On every such occasion, each member shall contribute towards the fund the sum of *sixpence*, for the purpose of replacing the said *five pounds* in the box; and, in the event of any overplus, it is hereby agreed to be given to the person entitled to receive it as above.

N. B. The *five pounds* shall be paid once, and no more, at the death of a wife or mother.

7. Should any member be shipwrecked, and lose his tools, he shall receive the sum of *one pound*, in order to enable him to replace the same.

8. No member of this society to assist in getting ships in or out of dock, without being paid for it. Any member being desired to work on a Sunday, to be paid double the usual wages per day.

9. Any member who may be working at a new ship, to have the same wages as at an old one, (allowance excepted.) When caulking a new ship, all the men employed at her to have the same allowance as those who are caulking.

10. When any member dies, his tools shall be brought to the club-room, and there publickly sold, for the benefit of the widow, if she be agreeable.

11. If any owner, or master of a ship, discharges any regular member of this society, through private pique, or any improper or insufficient reason, the rest of the men employed at the said ship will consider themselves bound to see justice done to the person aggrieved.

12. Two stewards, a clerk, and committee, to be chosen from the body of the members, at every six or twelve months, as may appear most satisfactory to the majority of the members. The money collected at each meeting to be deposited in the Savings' Bank, on the Saturday following; the stewards, or clerk, to make the deposits in the name of the society. and take a receipt for the same; which receipt must be exhibited to the committe at the next meeting, and filed, and the sum entered in the books of the society. The sum of *three shillings* and *sixpence* shall be allowed from the fund for expences at each committee meeting, when transacting business for the society.

13. The annual meeting of the members of this society shall be held on the 25th of December, at ten o'clock in the forenoon; when the accounts of the society shall be audited, officers elected for the ensuing year, and other special matters of the society taken into consideration. At this meeting it shall be lawful for a majority of the members to alter or rescind any of the foregoing rules, or to add new ones; which alterations, or additions, shall be entered into the society's book, and signed by the officers and committee, in behalf of the members.

14. It is hereby mutually agreed that, should any member be in want of men to work, he must employ those belonging to this society, in preference to others.

15. Any member using improper behaviour, or insolent and unbecoming language to his employer or employers, shall not be countenanced in any manner by this society.

North Shields, June 3rd, 1824.

BARNES & CO., PRINTERS.

15. 1824. Shipwrights' Union Society, North Shields.

"England expects every Man to do his Duty."

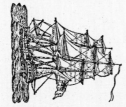

What a Pity Ship should be of able   *that a good upset for want Seamen ! !*

A DIALOGUE

Between Two Seamen, in North Shields.

Tom. GOOD MORNING, Harry! Have you seen a Hand Bill published by the Members of a New Union, established at the Commercial Hotel, Howard Street, North Shields?

Harry. Yes, Tom, I have just been reading it.

Tom. What do you think of it, Harry?

Harry. Think of it—I think very little of it, Tom. I like the Seamens' Union (as they call it) much better, and if I do enter one, I will enter the latter. The new one only proposes *Four Pounds* during the Winter Months, and *Three Pounds* in Summer, per Voyage; and only *Three Pounds* per Month, and no Benefits for its Members either for Shipwrecks or Deaths. The Seamens' Union proposes *Five Pounds* in Winter, *Four Pounds* in Summer, and the Monthly Wages in proportion; and should their Members be shipwrecked, and loss all their Clothes, they are paid *Five Pounds;* or if a Member die his Widow receives *Five Pounds,* and several other Benefits they are entitled to.

Tom. And does the New Union propose no Benefits to their Members, Harry?

Harry. There is only one I think.

Tom. What is that, Harry?

Harry. I can hardly tell you for laughing, Tom; they say they will protect their Members!

Tom. Protect their Members, Harry. When did the Press break out?

Harry. That's more than I can tell, Tom.

Tom. We protect no Members in our Society, every Member must protect himself.

Harry. That's the Society for me, Tom. I will not be many Minutes before I am a Member of it; and I hope every Seaman in the Kingdom will follow my example. So good Morning, to you, Tom.

Tom. Good Morning, to you, Harry; and I hope you will be a faithful Member, and fulfil all its Rules, &c. &c.

Harry. Let me alone for that, Tom. I will forfeit *Twenty Shillings* if I break any of its Rules. So, good Morning, once more, Tom.

Tom. Do not be in such a hurry, Harry. I have something more to say. Do not you think it a mean action for the New Union to entice the Members from the Old One?

Harry. I think it very mean, Tom; but I suppose they cannot get any Members but what are in some other Society, Tom.

Tom. So I think, Harry, and I believe they attempted last Year to establish a Union of Carpenters at the same place, but did not succeed in their attempt.

God save the King !!!

North Shields, February 14th, 1825.

16. 1825, anon.

TERMS OF AGREEMENT MADE

BETWEEN THE

Woollen Manufacturers

AND

THE WEAVERS' UNION

THAT the Weavers' Union shall concede the Point in dispute, relative to its interference in Mills and with Improved Machinery;—and the Manufacturers engage, that any person employed to spin on an Improved Power Machine, shall be enabled to earn, on the average, as much as a Slubber can on a large Billy, which is, at the present, from 22s. to 24s. per Week.

That the Union shall not interfere in the Internal Regulation of Hand-Loom-Shops, further than as regards the payment of the Statement Price of Wages, of 1824; and, that it shall not interfere between any Manufacturer and the Makers in his employ.

That the Union shall be conducted on Free Principles, and no Intimidations, Threats or Violence, shall be used to compel, but, that any Lawful means may be taken to prevail on persons to join it;—and, that no Manufacturer shall object to any Weaver or Spinner, on account of his or her joining it.

That no Turn-out shall take place, or be supported by the Union, against any Manufacturer, before the particulars of the Grievance have been stated in writing to the Manufacturers' Secretary, at least one week before such intended Strike shall take place:—and further, the Union has no intention of enforcing the repayment of any expenses incurred by a Strike against a Manufacturer, but, that any determination, relative to such Strike, shall be made by mutual consent of Manufacturers and Weavers.

In proof that the Union does not encourage any Intimidations or Threats, to be put in execution, in order to compel any person to comply in supporting it:—It offers £5. to be paid out of its fund, in conjunction with an equal sum from the Manufacturers, as a reward to those who will give information (so as to lead to conviction) against any individual or individuals, who shall, in future, commit violence on any one's person or property.

By order and on behalf of the Meeting of Manufacturers.

EDWARD CLEGG, Chairman.

Deputation of the Weavers' Union, with full authority to act on its behalf.
{ *John Crossley,*
James Buckley,
Edward Clegg,
Robert Lees. }

Rochdale, March 4th, 1828.

HARTLEY, PRINTER, ROCHDALE.

17. 1828. Weavers' Union, Rochdale.

18. 1832. Sheffield Typographical Society.

UNIONS.

Briercliffe & Burnley

Political

UNIONS.

The Public are informed that the above Unions
meet regularly once a fortnight, viz. the

BRIERCLIFFE

UNION meets at the Hare and Hounds Inn, HAGGATE, on
Tuesday Nights, at 7 o'clock, and the

BURNLEY

UNION at the Old Sparrow Hawk Inn, Burnley, on Monday
Nights at 7 o'clock, when all persons wishing to become Members are desired to attend, and where the objects and Laws of
the Political Unions may be seen, with a variety of Weekly
Political Publications from all parts of the Kingdom, where
political subjects are discussed, and from whence Petitions as
occasion may require, will be sent.

As equal Laws & Rights were ordained by the Almighty for
the Government of Society, we think that nothing less than
Annual Parliaments, Universal Suffrage, Vote by Ballot, and
No Property Qualification, can ever give permanent satisfaction to the community; for we assert, that all adult Persons,
except Criminals or Idiots, have a right to the Benefits of the
Elective Franchise. We are compelled to serve in the Wars,
and to pay Taxes, which, with the low Wages we get for our
labour, are at this moment sinking us, (the labouring classes)
to the lowest pitch of misery and ruin; thus we see our hard
earnings squandered by thousands of undeserving & ungrate-
ful persons, who in return have rendered us no beneficial service, either spiritual or temporal.

We therefore, with the consent of the Great National Union
of the working classes and others, pledge ourselves to petition
the Honorable House of Commons for a redress of our intol-
erable grievances.

JAS. NUTTALL, *Secretary.*

GOD SAVE THE KING.

Novr. 5th, 1832.

Earnshaw, Printer, &c. Colne.

19. 1832. Briercliffe & Burnley Political Unions.

NOTICE

To the Factory Children, their Parents and Friends.

THE

Public Meeting

Advertized to take place on **MONDAY, Sep. 29th**, in Ebenezer Chapel, Spring-Place, Huddersfield, for the Purpose of presenting

A BIBLE

TO THE

Rev. G. S. BULL,

(But which was postponed in Consequence of the Death of the Rev. Gentleman's Father,)

WILL TAKE PLACE

IN THE ABOVE CHAPEL,

ON MONDAY, OCTOBER 20th, 1834,

At Half-past Seven o'Clock in the Evening,

When the Friends of the above-named Gentleman, and especially the *Factory Children*, will have an opportunity of testifying their Gratitude to him, for his unwearied Labours in the Cause of the Poor, the Helpless, and the Distressed, by presenting him with the above Token of Respect.

Committee-Room, }
Oct. 13th, 1834. }   **JAS. BROOK, Secretary.**

N.B. All the Members of the Short Time Committee, are requested to attend a Special Meeting, at the White Hart Inn, on Saturday Evening, October 18th, at Eight o'Clock.

20. 1833. Huddersfield Short-Time Committee.

Trades' Unions

On Saturday, April 26th, orders were issued from the different Lodges of the Trades' Unions at Derby that the *Union was dissolved*, the funds of which had latterly been very rapidly on the decline; accordingly, on the Monday following, several hundred persons made application at the various Manufactories for employment, but in consequence of the many fresh hands that had been taken on from their having attached themselves to the Union not a fourth part were engaged, and it is calculated that upwards of *six hundred* are thus compelled to seek for employment in other places.

21. 1834. Grand National Consolidated Trade Union.

CAUTION.

WHEREAS it has been represented to us from several quarters, that mischievous and designing Persons have been for some time past, endeavouring to induce, and have induced, many Labourers in various Parishes in this County, to attend Meetings, and to enter into Illegal Societies or Unions, to which they bind themselves by unlawful oaths, administered secretly by Persons concealed, who artfully deceive the ignorant and unwary,---WE, the undersigned Justices think it our duty to give this Public Notice and Caution, that all Persons may know the danger they incur by entering into such Societies.

ANY PERSON who shall become a Member of such a Society, or take any Oath, or assent to any Test or Declaration not authorized by Law ---

Any Person who shall administer, or be present at, or consenting to the administering or taking any Unlawful Oath, or who shall cause such Oath to be administered, although not actually present at the time ---

Any Person who shall not reveal or discover any illegal Oath which may have been administered, although not actually present at the time ---

Any Person who shall not reveal or discover any illegal Oath which may have been administered, or any illegal Act done or to be done ---

Any Person who shall induce, or endeavour to persuade any other Person to become a Member of such Societies, WILL BECOME

Guilty of Felony,

and be liable to be

TRANSPORTED FOR SEVEN YEARS.

ANY PERSON who shall be compelled to take such an Oath, unless he shall declare the same within four days, together with the whole of what he shall know touching the same, will be liable to the same Penalty.

Any Person who shall directly or indirectly maintain correspondence or intercourse with such Society, will be deemed Guilty of an Unlawful Combination and Confederacy, and on Conviction before one Justice, on the oath of one Witness, be liable to a Penalty of TWENTY POUNDS, or to be committed to the Common Gaol or House of Correction, for THREE CALENDAR MONTHS; or if proceeded against by Indictment, may be CONVICTED OF FELONY, and be TRANSPORTED FOR SEVEN YEARS.

Any Person who shall knowingly permit any Meeting of any such Society to be held in any House, Building, or other Place, shall for the first offence be liable to the Penalty of FIVE POUNDS; and for every other offence committed after Conviction, be deemed Guilty of such Unlawful Combination and Confederacy, and on Conviction before one Justice, on the oath of one Witness, be liable to a Penalty of TWENTY POUNDS, or to Commitment to the Common Goal or House of Correction, FOR THREE CALENDAR MONTHS; or if proceeded against by Indictment may be

Convicted of Felony, and Transported for SEVEN YEARS.

COUNTY OF DORSET.
WAREHAM DIVISION.

February 20th, 1834.

JOHN BOND.
JOHN H. CALCRAFT.
JAMES C. FYLER.
GEORGE PICKARD, Junior.
NATHANIEL BOND.

C. Groves, Printer, Wareham.

22. 1834. The County of Dorset.

CAUSE OF FREEDOM!

The LONDON CENTRAL DORCHESTER COMMITTEE feel great pleasure in informing their Fellow-Workmen and all Enemies to Oppression, that a

PUBLIC DINNER

WILL TAKE PLACE AT

WHITE CONDUIT HOUSE,
ON

Monday, April 25, 1836,
IN

CELEBRATION OF THE REMISSION OF THE SENTENCE
ON THE

DORCHESTER LABOURERS,

And in Commemoration of the Moral Power displayed by the Working Classes of London in their great Procession, April, 1834.

T. WAKLEY, ESQ. M.P.

WILL PRESIDE.

COMMITTEE OF MANAGEMENT.

Messrs. T. BAKER.   J. BROWN.   W. ISAACS.   G. TOMEY.   J. RICHES.   T. PEAK.

LONDON DORCHESTER CENTRAL COMMITTEE.

Mr. W. ISAACS, 7, Saffron Street, Saffron Hill	Mr. PRICE, 2, Bath Place, Portland Street, Walworth
— T. BAKER, Young's Coffee House, 77, Curtain Rd.	— SIMPSON, Elm Cottage, Waterloo Street, Camberwell
— G. TOMEY, 33, Little Russell Street, Bloomsbury	— PHILLIPS, Cock, Camberwell
— J. RICHES, 11, Marmaduke Court, John Street, St. George's East	— WENLOCK, Horse and Groom, Gresse Street, Rathbone Place
— J. DAY, 1, Linton's Place, Limehouse Lock	— GARDINER, 5, Petty's Ct., Hanway, St., Oxford St.
— J. WHARTNABY, 61, John St., Blackfriars Road	— T. PEAK, 8, James Street, Stepney
— WINN, 11, Hatfield Place, Cross Street, Broadwall	— R. LOVELESS, 44, Paddington St., Marylebone
— WALKER, 6, Marlborough Street, New Cut	— BUSH, 9, Church Street, Kennington
— BURKINYOUNG, 2, Richmond Place, East Lane, Walworth	— LAKE, 1, Bedford Street, Walworth
— BROWN, 91, Leather Lane	— R. HARTWELL, (Secretary), 35, Brooke Street, West Square, Lambeth
— BARNES, 1, Collingwood Street, Camberwell	

STEWARDS.

Mr. W. D. SAULL, (Treasurer), 15, Aldersgate Street	Mr. PARTRIDGE, 3, Summers Street, Clerkenwell
Rev. Dr. WADE, 8, Trellick Terrace, Pimlico	— JOHN BELL, New True Sun Office, Bride Lane
Mr. A. H. BEAUMONT, 24, Brompton Square	— PETERS, White Conduit House
— J. ROBERTS BLACK, M.D., Chelsea	— HAMILTON, 4, West Street, Globe Fields
— W. HOARE, 1, Somers Place, New Road	— WOOSTER, 31, Ashford Street, Hoxton
— G. SIMKINS, 9, Stephen St., Tottenham Court Rd.	— J. ROBERTS, 25, Robert Street, Hampstead Road
— G. NORMAN, ditto	— TAPSON, 17, Clifton Street North, Finsbury
— HAYNES, 4, Princes Street, Stepney Green	— TALBOT, 9, Bedford St., Commercial Place, City Road (East)
— WILKINSON, 28, Trafalgar Street, Walworth	

Tickets 2s. 6d. each.—Double Tickets { To admit a Lady and Gentleman } 4s. 6d.

Tickets may be obtained of the Stewards and Committee as above; at the Committee Room, Turk's Head, King Street, Holborn; at the Bar of White Conduit House; and at the following places:

RISING SUN, East Lane, Walworth	DUKE OF WELLINGTON, High Street, Shoreditch
ROSE AND CROWN, Colville Court, Charlotte Street, Fitzroy Square	FOX AND GOOSE, Bermondsey Street
PEMBLEY'S COFFEE HOUSE, 62, John Street, Tottenham Court Road	STAR COFFEE HOUSE, William Street, Hampstead Road
LOVETT'S COFFEE HOUSE, 19, Greville Street, Hatton Garden	WESTMINSTER LITERARY INSTITUTION, Grosvenor Street, Millbank
MECHANICS' INSTITUTION TAVERN, Circus Street, New Road	Mr. WATSON, Publisher, 18, Commercial Place, City Road

DINNER ON TABLE AT HALF-PAST TWO PRECISELY.

In the course of the Afternoon several appropriate Glees will be sung.

The whole arrangements of the day will be under the immediate superintendence of the London Dorchester Central Committee, who pledge themselves that nothing shall be wanting on their part to ensure the comfort and convenience of those who may assemble to celebrate the day; and they feel confident that their exertions will be ably seconded by Mr. Peters, the landlord. The Dinner will be served hot, of the best description, in the large Room of the Tavern, and will consist of every sort of Roast and Boiled Meats, Hams, Vegetables, Bread, Porter; Plumb Pudding, and Tarts.

The Committee of Management meet every Wednesday, at the Turk's Head, King Street, Holborn; also on Monday and Saturday evenings, April 18 and 23, to issue Tickets and receive Money for those sold.

A

CONCERT AND BALL

In the Evening, in aid of the Fund for the support of the Wives and Families of the Dorchester Labourers,

UNDER THE DIRECTION OF MR. T. BUCKINGHAM,

Assisted by the following Ladies and Gentlemen:

Mr. T. JONES; Mr. BARTLEMAN; Mr. SCOTT; Mr. PARRY; Mr. BUCKINGHAM; HERR VON JOEL; Mrs. FITZGERALD; and Miss STEPHENS.

THE MUSICAL ARRANGEMENTS BY Mr. TINNEY.

THE BALL,

For which an excellent Band is engaged,

WILL BE CONDUCTED BY A PROFESSIONAL GENTLEMAN.

Tickets may be obtained at the Bar of White Conduit House, or of any Member of the Committee.

23. 1836. London Central Dorchester Committee.

The struggle for recognition

The failure of the Grand National Consolidated Trade Union and general unionism, and the setback of the Tolpuddle trial did not prevent the development of trade unionism among Britain's growing industrial workforce and the older craft unions. Throughout the country workers combined together to resist cuts in wages and to improve their conditions but their activities were more muted than before. Many craft organisations consolidated their craft practices, centralised their funds and amalgamated. Some unions developed a federal structure in order to eliminate the corruption that had bedevilled some of their organisations in the preceding years and a few began to engage full-time officials for the first time.

On the broader political front many workers, especially from among the skilled trades, became involved in Chartism, the most important popular political movement of the 1840s. Chartism, which started life in the London Working Men's Association in 1837, proposed a radical political platform based on a six-point charter: universal male suffrage, equal electoral districts, annual parliaments, payment of MPs, secret ballots and no property qualifications for MPs. But from the beginning the movement divided around class lines. On the one side ranged the skilled craftsmen and their middle-class supporters from London and the south who advocated 'moral force' – petitions, meetings, resolutions and education; and on the other were those, mostly from Wales and the north, who advocated 'physical force' including insurrection. Petitions to Parliament were tried without success. General strikes were proposed but rejected. An uprising in South Wales in November 1839 was quickly suppressed and the local leaders imprisoned. Briefly in 1842 in the north, the Midlands and Scotland Chartism became the rallying cry of the 'Plug Plot Rioters' (striking workers removed plugs from boilers to prevent them from working) but internal dissension and state repression broke the movement; there were 1,500 arrests and seventy-nine workers were transported.

Towards the end of 1842 the relationship between Chartism and the trade union movement was briefly consolidated by the founding of the Miners' Association of Great Britain and Ireland with several prominent Chartists in its leadership. The Miners' Association brought together men from every coalfield in Britain and at its peak in 1844 counted 60,000 pitmen as members. However, after a series of strikes aimed at improving wages and conditions, and ridding the industry of the hated bond system that tied men to yearly contracts, the employers finally broke the union by using blacklegs, soldiers and the police.

While the defeat of the miners was a setback for trade unionism it failed to deflect Chartism seriously from its political aims and many trade unionists continued to organise themselves under Chartism's banner. In April 1848 yet another attempt, accompanied this time by a massive demonstration, was made to present to Parliament a petition supporting the 'Six Points'. As on previous occasions the plan was rejected by a government that continued to see Chartism as an 'attack on property and civilised society' and, even worse, an attempt at the 'socialist restructuring of society'. In the ensuing months several Chartist leaders were arrested and imprisoned for conspiracy and within four years the movement had collapsed as an effective political force. In 1851, as though in celebration, Queen Victoria opened the Great Exhibition that trumpeted a Britain built on a free market for goods and labour, which in truth, as many knew to their cost, was built on cheap coal, cheap labour and the very limited political and social rights of the majority.

By the 1850s the number of trade unionists in Britain had grown to about 200,000 out of a total population of about 18 million. The nature of their organisations varied greatly depending on region, trade and local history. However, in most cases trade unions of this period comprised skilled and semi-skilled men with few women being members or organising separately. Unlike in previous decades, militancy and strikes were increasingly eschewed as unions fought to obtain respectability and extend their legal rights to organise. The carpenters, engineers, bricklayers and ironfounders all formed amalgamated societies and the powerful London Trades Council formed a 'Junta' to press for more moderation in union affairs. 'Strikes have been the bane of Trade Unionism' declared one union leader, while another stated that 'Strikes are to the social world what wars are to the political world. They become crimes unless they are prompted by absolute necessity' – a view much canvassed in a society which was increasingly coming to accept that trade unions were no longer a restraint on trade and that they had a positive role to play in determining wage levels. However, strikes and other forms of industrial action continued and as a result the courts continued to prosecute trade unionists using the 1825 legislation until finally in 1867 the government set up a Royal Commission to look at whether the very precarious legal status of trade unions and their funds could or should be changed.

When the commission came to take evidence it became apparent that the trade union movement lacked a single genuinely representative body with which it could speak. Two *ad hoc* committees existed; the 'Junta'-dominated Committee of Amalgamated Trades and the more militant St Martin's Hall Conference Committee, both based in London. Meanwhile in Manchester the idea of a single congress of trades unions was born when in February 1867 the Manchester and Salford Trades Council circulated an invitation for a 'Proposed Congress of Trades Councils' to discuss the 'probability of an attempt being made by the present Legislature, during the present session of Parliament, to introduce a measure detrimental to the interests of such Societies'. From the beginning the Congress was planned as an annual event with the first being held at Mechanics' Institute in Manchester in June and attended by thirty-four delegates representing some 118,000 trade union members. The London Trades Council and the 'Junta' both decided to cold shoulder the meeting seeing it as a potential rival to their own authority despite the Congress pledging itself to aid them in their 'laudable efforts to secure the legal protection of trade societies' funds' and their 'endeavours to amend the law in regard to conspiracy, intimidation, picketing, coercion, etc., which is . . . capable of misconstruction that it is utterly impossible that justice can be done'. The Congress also passed a resolution that it should 'take action in all Parliamentary matters pertaining to the general interests of the working class'.

When the Royal Commission finally reported it was clear that many of the old prejudices about trade unions as potentially violent organisations still persisted. The Majority Report viewed them in this way and recommended that trade unions should only be able to protect their funds under friendly society rules as long as they were peaceful and separated their strike and benefit funds. A Minority Report simply urged that trade unions should be legalised without conditions. In 1871 the government brought forward a single bill that attempted to reconcile these two contradictory opinions. On the one hand it proposed that the funds of registered unions should be protected and that restraint on trade was no longer to be seen as a criminal conspiracy. On the other, the bill retained much of the 1825 Act by keeping in clauses that made intimidation, obstruction and molestation criminal offences. The trade unions, desperate to appear respectable and orderly organisations, strongly objected to the inclusion of 1825 clauses and this resulted in the government splitting the bill into two and placing the criminal clauses into a separate Criminal Law Amendment Bill. Both pieces of legislation quickly passed into law.

Over the next several years campaigns against the Criminal Law Amendment Act unified the trade union movement as never before and following another Royal Commission the hated Act was repealed in 1875. Several other pieces of legislation that affected trade unions – like the Master and Servant Act and the Conspiracy and Protection Act – were either amended or enacted. Finally, in 1876, the 1871 Trade Union Act itself was amended, achieving what the Minority Report of the 1867 Royal Commission had wanted all along – legal trade unions where an action carried out by a worker in a union was no different in law from the same action carried out by any individual who was not a member of a union.

Meanwhile, the failure of the 1867 Reform Bill to achieve full manhood suffrage spurred many trade unionists to become involved in parliamentary politics so as to better represent the interests of the working classes. The newly established Trades Union Congress established a Parliamentary Committee in 1871 while several prominent trade union leaders stood as Liberals in parliamentary elections with mixed success.

The mid-1870s saw the setting in of the 'Great Depression' that was to have a serious effect on the newly recognised trade union movement, causing membership to decline rapidly particularly among those organisations which were newly established, for example in agriculture and the railways. Most unions survived but it was unemployment that was to concentrate their minds through much of the coming decades.

CHARTIST DEMONSTRATION!!

"PEACE and ORDER" is our MOTTO!

TO THE WORKING MEN OF LONDON.

Fellow Men,—The Press having misrepresented and vilified us and our intentions, the Demonstration Committee therefore consider it to be their duty to state that the grievances of us (the Working Classes) are deep and our demands just. We and our families are pining in misery, want, and starvation! We demand a fair day's wages for a fair day's work! We are the slaves of capital—we demand protection to our labour. We are political serfs—we demand to be free. We therefore invite all well disposed to join in our peaceful procession on

MONDAY NEXT, April 10,

As it is for the good of all that we seek to remove the evils under which we groan.

The following are the places of Meeting of THE CHARTISTS, THE TRADES, THE IRISH CONFEDERATE & REPEAL BODIES:

East Division on Stepney Green at 8 o'clock; City and Finsbury Division on Clerkenwell Green at 9 o'clock; West Division in Russell Square at 9 o'clock; and the South Division in Peckham Fields at 9 o'clock, and proceed from thence to Kennington Common.

Signed on behalf of the Committee, JOHN ARNOTT, Sec.

Henry Mitchener, Printer, 3, Edward Street, Hampstead Road.]

24. 1848. National Charter Association.

The Posters 1840–1880

The posters in this section show something of how radical politics affected trade union struggles for reform and justice among groups as far apart as miners in the north-east in the 1840s and the agricultural workers in the south in the 1870s. Victories were gained on the issues of recognition and the extension of the franchise for some working-class men.

(24) Chartism was the great political force of the 1840s and many trade unionists were engaged in its radical activities including the April 1848 mass demonstration and the planned march to Parliament to present a petition demanding political change. So fearful was the government of the demonstration that it fortified the area around Parliament and the royal palaces with thousands of troops and some artillery. On the day the government allowed the 150,000 Chartists and their supporters to assemble south of the Thames on Kennington Common: only the leaders were permitted across the fortified bridges to Westminster.

(25–32, 34, 35) The coal mines of Durham and Northumberland were dangerous and often deadly places to work and mine workers constantly campaigned for improvements in their conditions but their pleas to the government and the coal owners often fell on deaf ears. Coal owners like the Marquis of Londonderry – one time aide-de-camp to the Duke of Wellington, Lord of the Bedchamber to George IV, duellist and reactionary Tory Lord Lieutenant of Durham – cared little for the plight of the men who worked his mines. In 1844 the short-lived Miners' Association of Great Britain and Ireland pressed for better wages and conditions: Londonderry brought in blacklegs, intimidated local shopkeepers and threatened the union with the law. In 1854 his son, the fourth marquis, was still refusing to pay adequate wages to miners at his Seaton pit, forcing them out on strike, but by this time the miners had no union to defend their interests and had to appeal to the public to support their cause.

(33) In September 1841, a year after building work on the new Houses of Parliament had begun, the masons came out on strike protesting against constant bullying by one the contractor's foremen, George Allen. Allen, the masons claimed, was 'a man who damns and blasts and curses at every turn' and 'daily commits acts of tyranny and oppression'. The contractor, Grissell and Peto, was unmoved, believing Allen's job was to run the site with 'the discipline of the quarterdeck'. The masons' response was 'that the employers not only expected to purchase the labour of a man but also his soul'. The dispute dragged on for eight months until a combination of blacklegs, a press campaign and open government support for the contractors finally forced the masons back to work.

(36, 37) Piece work was often a way of cutting wages and when, in the mid-1850s, the Coventry ribbon manufacturer J.J. Cash argued it was the only way to beat foreign competition, the workers replied with an elegant criticism on the nature of capitalism (see also 200).

(38) George Potter, the militant editor of the labour journal *Beehive* and leader of the London building workers, marshalled the peaceful mass demonstration of trade unionists to Hyde Park in 1866 and his conduct of the event helped persuade the Conservative government that skilled, urban, working-class men could be trusted with the vote which they were subsequently granted in the 1867 Reform Act.

(39) While the situation of the skilled urban worker was improving in the 1860s, the plight of the unenfranchised agricultural labourer was still desperate as these Buckinghamshire labourers argued. For many the way out was to move into towns or even to emigrate to the colonies.

(40) Newcastle compositors told a familiar story of the 'oppressive tyranny' of a new newspaper proprietor changing working practices in order to drive down wages.

(41) After four years of campaigning the London Trades Council and the TUC succeeded in getting the 1871 Criminal Law Amendment Act repealed. The Act had made picketing illegal and trade unionists vulnerable to prosecution despite unions being recognised as lawful under the Trade Union Act of 1871.

(42, 43) Since 1869 the Labour Representation League had tried to get working-class men elected to Parliament and the 1874 election saw their first success. Two miners, Alexander Macdonald and Thomas Burt, took their seats on the Liberal benches. The well-known radical Charles Bradlaugh, although elected in 1880, was denied his seat because he was an atheist. Lloyd Jones was a leading figure of the Co-operative Union.

(44, 45) Since their beginnings trade unions have found themselves rebutting rumours, particularly during strikes. They have always been accused of being bent on violence to gain their ends and suffered allegations that their leaders were corrupt and 'living in clover', as this rebuttal from the Wigan Miners' Association shows.

(46) In 1872 the Warwickshire farm labourer and Methodist preacher Joseph Arch founded the National Agricultural Labourers' Union and within a year the organisation had 100,000 members. In the following three years, in the face of great hostility from squires, the union managed to raise wages only to see them fall back as farmers locked out workers and farm produce prices fell.

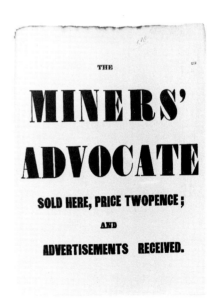

THE

MINERS' ADVOCATE

SOLD HERE, PRICE TWOPENCE;

AND

ADVERTISEMENTS RECEIVED.

25. 1843. Miners' Association of Great Britain and Ireland.

THE
PITMEN'S
PETITION.

" **To the Honourable the Commons of the United Kingdom of Great Britain and Ireland, in Parliament assembled.**

" **The Petition of the Undersigned Pitmen, who work in the Coal Mines of Durham and Northumberland,** *unanimous adopted at a Public Meeting, held on the Black Fell, February,* *May 13, 1841,*

☞ HUMBLY SHEWETH, —

"That within the last TWENTY *26* YEARS upwards of SEVEN HUNDRED *700* PITMEN, the friends and companions of your Petitioners, HAVE BEEN MISERABLY DESTROYED IN THE DURHAM AND NORTHUMBERLAND MINES, BY EXPLOSIONS OF INFLAMMABLE GAS ; and that, in addition, great numbers more, from various other causes, have also encountered in the same Mines the most fearful deaths.

"That the cause of those fearful Explosions is invariably THE WANT OF SUFFICIENT VENTILATION, which permits the accumulation of Inflammable Gas or *Fire Damp* from the Coal in such large masses, that, accidently set fire to, explode with such tremendous force as sometimes to blow men through the shaft 200 yards deep, as if from a cannon mouth, and shake the solid structure of the Earth in the neighbourhood of the Pit, as if with an Earthquake.

"That the lives of your Petitioners are not a day or an hour secure from such deadly operations ; and that it is a horrible and fearful thing to die such a death, or live in daily expectation of.

That in addition to the destruction by these sudden calamities, insufficient ventilation produces a vitiated mining atmosphere, from the poisonous Gases and dampness of the Mines, in which from ten to twelve hours a day your Petitioners are confined, breathing it under a severity of labour seldom practised on the surface, which brings on suffering, emaciation, disease, and early death.

"That in every case of Explosion of late years, it has been demonstrated beyond doubt, by the evidence at the Coroners' Inquests, that *imperfect ventilation*, and *that alone*, brought on the dreadful catastrophe ; as at St. Hilda Explosion, in June, 1839, in which 52 lives were lost ; at Willington, in April, 1841, in which 32 ; at Thornley Pit, in August, 1841, in which 9 ; and at King Pit, in April, of the present year (1843), in which 28 lives were thus destroyed.

"That your Petitioners are clearly convinced that while Mines are allowed to be worked as at present with only a *single-bratticed Pit* to each, as in the greatest number of instances in these districts, through which are supplied 100, 200, 300, 400, and sometimes 500 acres of underground workings, extending in some cases to 60 or 70 miles of passages, that the lives of your Petitioners will continue in daily imminent danger, from the *incapacity of one Shaft to supply a sufficient quantity of air*. That your Petitioners are further convinced that *bratticed Shafts*, or Pits divided by wooden partitions, are very imperfect, dangerous, and ill-fitted for securing proper ventilation, as they waste the air at its source by allowing an escape from the *downcast* to the *upcast*, through a wooden partition of about seven inches thick, the temperature differing between them from 50† to 60†; that in accidents they get easily deranged or destroyed ; and, as is universally the case where they exist, are used at the same time for drawing Coals in Corves or Tubs, which obstruct, by the amount of their areas, the admission and egress of air in their already too-diminished capacities.

"That the only mode of securing proper ventilation, whatever direct means may be employed for producing it, *is by sinking* TWO SHAFTS *always to the coal or winning*, and, *in proportion as the underground workings are extended*, MAKING ADDITIONAL SHAFTS ; and thus would the whole Mine be thoroughly ventilated, the Coal more easily and healthily worked, and your Petitioners secured from the recurrence of these terrible accidents.

"That Your Petitioners, knowing that the *Davy Lamp is liable to fire an explosive mixture under certain circumstances*, cannot rest satisfied with their lives being secured only by *an imperfect instrument*, easily deranged, which at the moment of greatest danger develops its imperfection and brings on the mischief it is intended to prevent, and on the pretended safety of which has been based the modern practice of carrying foul underground workings to the most dangerous extent, demonstrating, your Petitioners humbly hope, to your Honourable House, another important reason for the adoption of an efficient ventilation.

"That such ventilation may be properly applied, and the Mine placed in every respect in as perfect a condition as its nature will admit, your Petitioners respectfully submit to your Honourable House, that means should be adopted to secure, for the direction of the Mines, *Viewers and Underviewers properly educated and sufficiently experienced* for their onerous charge, to whose care lives as well as much valuable property are entrusted, and by whose ignorance they are not unfrequently sacrificed ; and your Petitioners consider it only proper, as in other professions, so in that of mining, *that a scientific and suitable education should be possessed by the Officers* of Mines, previous to the assumption of their important duties—which should be made imperative.

"That for the securing of these and other improvements and advantages to the Mines, which self-interest or negligence might resist, evade, or leave unaccomplished, even though authorized by your Honourable House, your Petitioners conceive that the *appointment of official Inspectors of Mines*, as of Factories and Railways, with authority to investigate, suggest, and recommend or enforce, would greatly conduce thereto, and, also, to their early introduction and right-working.

"The adoption of these suggestions, your Petitioners are firmly convinced, is imperatively necessary for providing against the dreadful calamities of the Mines, and for their better and economical working, your Petitioners, therefore, humbly and most earnestly pray that your Honourable House will take them, and any other beneficial suggestions that may be made, into your immediate and serious consideration. And should your Honourable House, induced by the importance of the subject to humanity and the interests of the country, favourably incline to this their faithful representation, your Petitioners further humbly and respectfully pray that, for obtaining more particular and extensive information on all points bearing on the Mines and receiving confirmation of the facts stated in the premises, your Honourable House will be pleased to appoint a Select Committee of Inquiry, or take such steps as may be necessary for the appointment of a *Commission of Scientific and Practical Men to visit the Mines and investigate their condition by personal inquiry and examination*, with a view to speedily report thereon, for the purpose of basing a practical, complete, and comprehensive measure, by which your Petitioners may, for the future, be better protected from the fearful destruction that is perpetually carrying death and woe into the bosoms of their families.

"And your Petitioners, as in duty bound, will ever pray, &c."

May, 1843.

H. M'COLL, PRINTER, 5, KING STREET, SOUTH SHIELDS.

26. 1843. Miners' Association of Great Britain and Ireland.

CAUTION

TO

PITMEN.

The Statute of the 6th Geo. 4th, c. 129. Section 3, enacts, that if any person shall, by violence to the person or property, or by threats or intimidation, or by molesting, or in any way obstructing another, force or endeavour to force any person hired or employed, to depart from his hiring, employment or work, or prevent or endeavour to prevent any person, not hired or employed, from hiring himself, or accepting work or employment. Or if any person shall, by the same means, force or induce another to belong to any club or association, or force or endeavour to force any person carrying on any trade or business, to make any alteration in his mode of regulating, managing, conducting, or carrying on such trade or business, or to limit the number or description of his workmen, or servants, every person so offending or aiding, abetting, or assisting therein, being convicted thereof, shall and may be imprisoned and kept to hard labour for any time not exceeding three calendar months.

And the statute 9th Geo. 4th, c. 31 Sec. 25, enacts, that if any person shall be charged with, and convicted of, any assault committed in pursuance of a conspiracy to raise the rate of wages, the court may sentence the offender to be imprisoned, with or without hard labour, in the common Gaol or House of Correction, for any term not exceeding 2 Years, and may also, if it shall so think fit, fine the offender, and require him to find sureties for keeping the peace.

May, 1844.

From J. Procter's Office, High Street, Hartlepool.

27. 1844. Her Majesty's Government.

PITMEN'S STRIKE.

Holdernesse House, July 3, 1844.

I once more, and for the last time address you. The most deluded and obstinate victims of designing men and crafty Attorneys must now perceive (after twelve weeks' strike) that they cannot become masters and dictate terms to the Coal-owners. Already 3639 men are employed (principally Strangers to the Districts of Northumberland and Durham) in hewing coals; 766 sensible men have left the Union and returned to work. The produce of their labour is 5177 chaldrons per day. And, with this positive fact before your eyes, and with more strangers coming forward daily, is it possible, the old, respectable, well-thinking colliers can be so infatuated as to suppose, by still standing out in rebellion, that they can conquer their employers?
Pitmen! I enjoin! I conjure you! to look upon the ruin you are bringing on your wives, your children, your county, and the country, In twelve weeks more the collieries will be peopled by foreigners, and you will have neither shelter, protection, or work. While their is yet time---reflect!! I will give you all, hitherto in my employment, *one more trial*. I have been amongst you---I have reasoned---I have pointed out to you the folly, the misery, the destruction awaiting you, by your stupid and most insane union. I gave you two weeks to consider whether you would return to your work, before I proceeded to eject you from your houses. I returned to Pensher, and I found you dogged, obstinate, and determined---indifferent to my really paternal advice and kind feelings to the old families of the Vane and Tempest pitmen who had worked for successive ages in the mines. I was bound to act up to my word---bound by duty to my property, my family, and station. I superintended then many ejectments---it had no avail. I warned you next I would bring over workmen from my Irish estates, and turn more men out---you heeded me not. I have now brought Forty Irishmen to the pits; and I will give you all *one more week's notice*. And if by the 13th of this month a large body of my pitmen do not return to their labour, I will obtain one hundred more men, and proceed to eject that number, who now are illegally and unjustly in possession of my houses; and in the following week another one hundred shall follow. I will be on the spot myself; the civil and military power will be at hand to protect the good men and the strangers; and you may rely upon it the majesty of the law, and the rights of property, will be protected and prevail.

Believe me, I am, your sincere friend,

VANE LONDONDERRY.

Wm. Heaton, Printer, Newcastle.

28. 1844. The Marquis of Londonderry.

TO THE DECEIVED AND DELUDED

WORKMEN

NOW EMPLOYED ON THE COLLIERIES
IN NORTHUMBERLAND AND DURHAM.

FELLOW-MEN AND BRETHREN,—We, the Miners of Northumberland and Durham, from the protracted nature of the Strike, feel ourselves called upon to address YOU at this very critical juncture, more especially the men of our own counties who have given precedence and assistance to the infamous work of bringing strangers to supplant us. On YOU at this moment depends, in a very great degree, the salvation of 33,000 Men and Boys, who are manfully struggling for labour's rights, and on you the charge will rest of causing all the evils that may arise out of the present struggle ; your very act of going to work has, and continues to protract the Strike and keep up feelings of hostility between the Masters and their late Workmen. Are you aware of the evil you are doing, the misery you are creating, the hopes you are blasting, and the inevitable ruin you must bring upon yourselves, your families, your country, and on thousands yet unborn ? We call upon you then as with the voice of many waters, will you respond to our call, or will you continue deaf to all restraint ? We exhort you, we expostulate with you, come to our rescue, risk your present apparent interest for the sake of your country's emancipation, think no sacrifice too hard to make. The very act of responding to our call will be the salvation of your country. Have you any sympathy, any benevolence, any philanthropic feelings for suffering humanity ? If you have one drop of an Englishman's blood in your veins, we entreat you to cease doing the work of a factious and interested party. Join the ranks of our Association, and the right hand of fellowship will be given to you, and your interest will be considered as our own.

A word to religious men who are working. Suffer us to call your attention to our righteous struggle. Your character is at stake, if not nearly destroyed ; you may yet redeem it, and although you may have been caught unawares, nevertheless you ought not to continue to do evil that good may come of it ; you have already afflicted the Churches with whom you are identified ; many of your brethren have wept over you and for you, their confidence in you is for the present suspended, and they have been led to exclaim how has the fine gold become dim ; you have sowed dissension in almost every religious body in Northumberland and Durham, yea, the very act you have done has furnished our opponents with weapons the most powerful, though as yet unsuccessful. Look at the future happiness of suffering thousands, and the depressed state under which they groan. Are you destitute of feeling on their account ? if not there is yet a good hope. Rise to the rescue of your almost ruined Brethren, who are struggling manfully in labour's battle in defence of your rights and their own.

In conclusion, you have pierced the bosoms of the best of your friends with many sorrows. One day's calm reflection may redeem the confidence of your Friends, nay, a moment's thought may again shed the refulgent rays of peace throughout all channels of society. Brethren, respond to your country's call, we can yet be free.

Believe me yours, for the Miners of Northumberland and Durham,
and on behalf of the Committee,

EDW. RICHARDSON.

July 20th, 1844.

Newcastle-on-Tyne : T. DODDS, Printer, Miners' Advocate Office, 77, Side.

29. 1844. Miners' Association of Great Britain and Ireland.

MEANS AND WAYS!!!

READ! READ!!

" NOTICE.

"JULY 20th, 1844.

"THE MARQUIS OF LONDONDERRY has given orders that no person, Pitman or Workman, is to be permitted to come in his carriages, or any of their families, to Seaham Harbour, for the purposes of Marketing or Buying Goods, who are not *bona fide* at his work, and employed in his Collieries.

"LORD LONDONDERRY again warns all the Shopkeepers and Tradesmen in his town of Seaham, that if they still give credit to Pitmen who hold off work, and continue in the Union; such men will be marked by his Agents and Overmen, and will never be employed in his Collieries again; and the Shopkeepers may be assured that they will never have any Custom or Dealings with them from LORD LONDONDERRY's large Concerns, that he can in any manner prevent.

"LORD LONDONDERRY further informs the Traders and Shopkeepers, that having by his measures increased very largely the last Year's Trade to Seaham, that if Credit is so improperly, and so fatally given to his unreasonable Pitmen, thereby prolonging the injurious strike; it is his firm determination to carry back all the outlay of his Concerns, even to Newcastle.

"Because it is neither fair, just, or equitable that the resident Traders in his own Town should combine, and assist the Infatuated Workmen, and Pitmen, in prolonging their own miseries by continuing an Insane Strike, and an unjust and senseless Warfare against their Proprietors and Masters.

" Vane Londonderry."

SHOPKEEPERS

LOOK OUT!!!

READ AND JUDGE FOR YOURSELVES.

The above precious Production has been profusely circulated among the Shopkeepers of *Seaham Harbour*, and tells a fearful tale of Lordly influence, it also shows the *parental* and *benevolent* disposition that characterizes his Lordship! Can any Person *now* doubt that his Workmen have been kindly or humanely treated? or that under *such a Master* (and he is considered to be one of the best!) they should attempt to complain! There is tyranny of the blackest nature in the above Bill, besides it is illegal—he threatens and intimidates the Shopkeepers and Tradesmen!—he will MARK THEM!! Not only will he do "what he likes with his own," but he will dictate to others how they shall expend theirs! How generous and liberal! What would be said if the Unionists used language similar to the above? But then he is a Marquis, a Peer of the Realm, and Lord-Lieutenant of the County of Durham, while the other Parties are only *ignorant, senseless* Pitmen, and their Union, which numbers upwards of One Hundred Thousand Members, is an "*Insane Union!*" Of course, the Coal Owners' Union of which his Lordship is a worthy Member, *that* is a wise and honourable Union! His Lordship lately stated that his Workmen said to him (by Deputation), "That they had nothing whatever to complain of from me or my Viewers, but that they were *compelled* by the power and force of the Union to fight the Battle of others, who, they stated, were not well used like them." We deny this statement; there is not one particle of truth in the whole! His Lordship has surely forgot himself, or thinks we are poor, silly creatures who can swallow anything, and for whom any treatment is good enough! We thank him! He will not allow us to go to work without signing the Monthly Bond, and how will that operate with respect to Shopkeepers and Tradesmen? Why, the Workmen being at the *caprice* and *whim* of the Masters a continual turning off would take place each Month, a large number of Men would, consequently, always be idle. Shopkeepers can testify that the majority of Pitmen are always a Fortnight at least in Debt, therefore, should the Monthly Agreements be enforced they will most certainly be considerable losers thereby, and it is this knowledge of the obvious results that will follow the acceptance of such a Bond that has hitherto induced the Trades-people to support on credit, and by other means, the Industrious, Patient, yet insulted Miners of these two Counties. Truly the Shopkeepers and "the resident Traders in HIS OWN TOWN" deserve the pity and sympathy of their own Class throughout the Kingdom."

By Order of the Committee of his Lordship's late numerous and Honest Workmen,
The Miners of Pensher, Rainton, and Pittington Collieries,
Signed, on their Behalf,

EDW. RICHARDSON.

July 23nd, 1844.

N. B. The statement in the "Tyne Mercury," of this morning, that 47 Men had gone to work in the Marquis' Collieries is UNTRUE---only THREE of his old hands having returned to work.

Newcastle-on-Tyne: T. DODDS, Printer, Miners' Advocate Office, 77, Side.

30. 1844. Miners' Association of Great Britain and Ireland.

MINERS' NATIONAL CONFERENCE.

Union, Information, and Restriction of Labour are the Instruments that are destined to rescue the Miners of Great Britain from their present state of Thraldom and Oppression."—MINERS' ADVOCATE.

The Conference of Delegates belonging to the Miners' Association of Great Britain and Ireland will commence its sittings in Newcastle-upon-Tyne, on Monday, July 7th ; and consequently it has been agreed that a series of

Public Meetings

Will be held during the week, to be attended by Delegates from the different Mining Districts in Britain.

MEETINGS FOR THE TYNE COLLIERIES.

Meetings of the following Collieries will be held

On MONDAY, the 7th of July, 1845,

At the undermentioned places, viz.,

SCAFFOLD HILL,

For the men of West Moor, Earsdon, Six Mile Bridge, Backworth, Holywell, Percy Main, Wallsend, Willington, Heaton, Walker, and the other Collieries in the vicinity. This meeting will be addressed by Mr. WELSBY, from Lancashire, one of the Executive Council ; Mr. DANIELLS, Editor of the MINERS' ADVOCATE ; and Mr. J. FAWCETT. On the same day a Meeting will be held at

BOTANY BAY,

Near West Cramlington, for the men of West Cramlington, Seghill, Seaton Delavel, East Cramlington, Netherton, Whitley, and Cowpen ; to be addressed by Mr. DURD, one of the Executive Council for Yorkshire, Derby, Leicester, and Nottingham ; Mr. HARDY, and Mr. SCOTT. Another Meeting will be held on the same day at

SHERIFF HILL

For the men of Washington, Oxclose, Ravensworth, Pelton Fell, Ouston, Urpeth, Kibblesworth, Blaydon Main, King Pit, South Shields, Jarrow, Hebon, Brockley Whins, Friars Goose, Springwell, Heworth, Felling, and Oakwellgate ; to be addressed by Mr. M. JUDE, Mr. HOLGATE, from Yorkshire, and by Mr. PRICE, from Cheshire. Besides the above speakers the Meeting will be addressed by several Delegates from the different Mining Counties. Chair taken at each Meeting at Six o'Clock, P. M.

Printed at the Miners' Advocate Office, Sun Inn, Side, Newcastle.

READ THE MINERS' ADVOCATE

FOR SEPTEMBER, PRICE ONLY TWOPENCE.

Contents:

THE

Dreadful Explosion

At Jarrow, with remarks on the inquest and on the conduct of the Coroner. Restriction of Labour. Synopsis of Geography. On the elevation of the Working Classes. Explosions in mines. Sameness of Coroners' Inquests, and verdicts of Juries. T. S. Duncombe Esq., M. P. on Strikes &c. Origin of the coal trade. Wigan Miners. On the freedom of Man. Alfred the Great an advocate for Restricted Labour. Lecturers Reports. Original Poetry, on the Jarrow Explosion. Choice bits. Enigmas, Charades. Notes to Correspondents, &c., &c. To be had at the Advocate Office, Side, Mr. T. Horn, Music Seller, Messrs. P. France & Co., Booksellers, Side, Newcastle.

Printed at the Miners' Advocate Office, Sun Inn, Side, Newcastle.

31–2. 1845. Miners' Association of Great Britain and Ireland.

STRIKE
AT THE NEW
HOUSES OF PARLIAMENT.
Notice to the Public!

We, the Masons lately employed at the above works, having observed in the public papers of the Metropolis repeated attacks upon our character, relative to our recent strike, we therefore considered it our duty to defend ourselves through the same channel we were attacked; but to our surprise we found such channels only open to one side of the question, which must at once convince a discerning public that our opponents' position cannot be maintained by fair and just means. In consequence of a letter having appeared in the "Times" of Monday the 4th instant, signed Messrs Grissell and Peto, we felt ourselves called upon to answer the same through the medium of the same journal, and therefore sent the following letter, which was refused insertion, and which has also been refused by several of the daily press :—

(TO THE EDITOR OF THE TIMES.)

SIR,

A LETTER having appeared in the *Times* of this day, signed MESSRS. GRISSELL & PETO, stating that the charges made by the Masons lately employed at the New Houses of Parliament, against Mr. Allen, their foreman, are without the slightest foundation, and that the secession of the workmen has not originated in any oppression on the part of their foreman, we trust in your sense of justice to give insertion to the following reply in vindication of our rights as men, and to substantiate our charges:—

It would take up too much of your valuable space to enter *seriatim* into a refutation of their refutations; but, suffice it to say, that we regard them as mere glosses and evasions. Allen himself has not denied our charges, and Messrs. Grissell & Peto have merely made an attempt to shift the question, and to throw the blame upon what they are pleased to term our idleness and inexperience. This charge comes with an ill grace from them, after having posted bills on their own gates, declaring us to be sober and industrious.

We would also beg to remind Messrs. Grissell & Peto that they themselves virtually admitted the truth of our charges against Allen, for when we made a complaint to them on a former occasion they promised that Allen should alter his conduct. He did alter it. But how? He merely changed from one species of tyranny to another. He adopted the system of encouraging what they are pleased to term *chasing*, whereby one man who, might be gifted with greater physical ability than another, could be excited to do more work than his companions; his performance is then made a standard for the quantity of labour *demanded* from all the rest, who are bullied and abused if unable to come up to this mark.

We do not wish to have the nomination of our superintendant, but we wish that a tyrant might not be appointed; for no man, possessed with

a spark of manliness, can submit to have his feelings outraged in the manner which Allen is constantly doing. The public will bear in mind that we are not the first who have struck against this man's tyranny. The Masons of Birmingham struck against him in 1837, and Allen, we are sorry to say, has not mended in temper, if he has in circumstances.

In conclusion, we beg to reiterate our charges,—we could add to them, were we disposed to do so, and are prepared to prove them by the evidence of the sufferers and eye-witnesses of his tyranny. Instead of shrinking from them, we court public enquiry and investigation into them; we challenge it, and are ready at any convenient time and place to meet it.

It is not of the quantity of work required, or the rate of our wages, that we complain, but of the unbearable insolence and oppression of a taskmaster, who resembles those of Pharaoh; and who would reduce us to a bondage worse than that of the Egyptians; and because we complain of it, is it to be said—" Go to, ye are idle?"

We have all along separated our employers from the tyrannical foreman, for we believed that the conduct of the latter was not tolerated by them. We are therefore surprised and sorry to observe that they have now made common cause with him, and identified themselves with him. But they cannot justly constitute themselves arbitrators in their own case, any more than we in ours. All we want (and surely we do not ask too much) is that a more civil man than Allen be appointed as our superintendant, and in the mean time rest our cause upon the candid and impartial consideration of the public.

FROM THE OPERATIVE MASONS,

PAVIERS' ARMS, WESTMINSTER.

October 6th, 1841.

This has been thought unfit to appear in the "liberty loving" and impartial daily press of the metropolis. But mark their honesty: an article appeared in the columns of the *Times* of last week, containing the greatest amount of unprincipled falsehoods in so short a space it was ever our misfortune to behold. Mr. Jackson, of Pimlico, (to whom the said article principally alluded) was so disgusted with its audacious falsehoods, that he immediately contradicted it in the same Journal the following day, but nevertheless, it appeared in almost all the metropolitan press, both daily and weekly, although it must have been obvious to them all that they were promulgating the grossest falsehoods. Under these circumstances we have been forced to the alternative of placards, by which means we beg to state to Messrs. Grissell & Peto and the Public that we struck against a system the most degrading to the human character in existence. We have maintained our position hitherto peacefully and manfully; and however far they may have recourse to error and mystification—however far they try to persuade the public and us that injuries are not injuries, we have felt the lash, and have withdrawn from beneath its excruciating inflictions; and when they are prepared to remove the slave driver, then, and not till then, are we prepared to resume our employment. Resting our cause with an impartial public, we subscribe ourselves

Your humble Servants,

THE MASONS,
Lately employed at the New Houses of Parliament.

THOMAS CARTER, Sec.

SALISBURY & BATEMAN, Printers.

33. 1841. Operative Stonemasons' Society.

IMPORTANT TO

MINERS &c.

NOTICE,

A Public District Meeting will be held in a Field between **HASWELL** and **HETTON**, on Saturday, the 21st of May, 1853, to take into consideration the present Low Rate of Wages, the High Price of Provisions, and the Imperfect State of the Ventilation in many of the Collieries; also, the inadequacy of the present System of Mine Inspection.

CHAIR TAKEN at 2 O'CLOCK p.m.

Several well known Friends will address the Meeting.

FELLOW MEN,---you well know the sad condition you are now in. The wages of all classes of working men are on the advance, but not so with you. The cause rests with yourselves, want of union empowers your employers to plunder you as they choose. Attend then in your thousands as in times gone by. Show a bold front and a general muster, and thus testify that the spirit of 1831 and 1844 still lives, and will not submit to allow the employers to deprive you of that union which the laws of your country guarantee to you as a birth-right, and which you are bound as parents to hand down unjured to your children. Rally then around the standard of union, and demonstrate to your employers that as they combine to oppress you and reduce your wages, you will assert your rights to defend your labour, your only capital.

Union, union! let our watch word be,
And soon the oppressed shall be free.
Pray dont forget the important day,
The glorious 21st of May
Let music sound and banners fly,
Union we must have, or we die

BY ORDER OF THE DISTRICT MEETING.

W. BOSTLE AND SON, (Successors to T. Dodds,) PRINTERS, 61, GREY STREET, NEWCASTLE.

34. 1853. Miners' National Association.

TO THE
PUBLIC

The Men at Seaton Colliery having Struck on the 18th, of October, for the following advance of price:-

Hewing:- 1 Shilling per Score,

And 10 lbs. more put on to the Weight of Stones for the laid out.

They are still determined to have that advance and humbly thank the Public for the maintenance they have received from them, and crave a continuance of their sympathy.

Up Brother Miners, give your fears to the Winds, and let us break the bars of Tyranny, when wicked men conspire, honest men should unite, for Tyranny only casts her Anchor in the Sea of ignorance, let us unite and drive her on to the Rocks of everlasting despair, and may she never find a Pilot's repose.

Up with the Flag over Tyranny's dark Sea,
For the Miners and Seamen shall be free,
Rouse from your Slumbers ye sorrow bitten Slaves,
Freedom is Life, Slavery is Death.

Look here, Brother Miners, there are One Hundred and Seventeen Members at Seaton Colliery, and not one at work. Please to keep from this Colliery, and let us have a fair chance to gain our object. There are now **Several Families turned to the door,** and our Master says that he will not give us one farthing advance.

We have agreed to take 8d. in place of 1s. as above but the Masters still refuse.

We beg to inform our Friends that the Deputies, Stonemen, and Shifters, have joined the Union.

We remain Yours in the bonds of Unity,
The Men at Seaton Colliery

Seaton Colliery, Nov. 22nd, 1854.

35. 1854. Miners' National Association.

TO THE

FACTORY OPERATIVES

OF

Coventry and Surrounding Districts.

"Thrice is he armed that hath his quarrel just,"

Brother and sister Operatives,—The word is spoken, the fiat has gone forth, our employer has decreed that piece-work, not weekly wages, shall in his factory be the ruling order of the day. For thus it is, on the one hand stands the capitalist, on the other the labourer. Trade is brisk, provisions are high, but wages low. The Operative seeks by deputation for a slight advance for superior skill and industry, but is met by an ingenious and cunning devised system of piece-work. Workers you tread on each others heels, but will you tread on each others hearts, by seeking employment to supplant virtuous minded men, who have made this willing sacrifice rather than be made the instruments to carry out a plan that will destroy the happiness of domestic employment and scarce find oil sufficient to keep the human frame in working order? If not, now is the time to concentrate all your energies on the question. As intelligent men we conjure you to reflect on it, for it is calculated to reduce wages, to be injurious to the community, and most probably in a few years will concentrate the whole silk trade of Coventry into a few hands. The same competition that produces low wages produces low prices, for the sake of which, and of high profits, the low wages are paid. But, as competition keeps driving the prices down, it drives the profits down also, till at last the competition becomes so keen that those only can stand who have large capital, and whose wholesale manufacture admits of smaller profits by admitting of greater cheapness. Under this state of things the weakest goes to the wall, the small manufacturer is devoured by the large one, the curse rests in the employing class, who are by their selfish competition beginning, scorpion-like, to sting themselves. Shall the 200 women and men for want of sympathy and support, bow and tremble, while their employer is working off the last will of their golden thread to experimentalise on the sufferings of poor women and men. All eyes are directed to this important struggle which is doomed to establish the rights of labour and to stave off piece-work for an indefinite term. There must be a general advance of wages; let us endeavour to make this feeling universal. Our notices expire on Saturday next, when our motto will be "peace," "law," and "order," no personal ill feeling, clamour, or prejudice, but a desire to promote the just cause of labour, and the social happiness of women and men

By order of the Committee of the Operatives in the employ of Messrs. J. & J. Cash.

Printed by Taunton and Son, Auctioneers, Valuers, Shipping and Estate Agents, Burges, Coventry.

No 1

1/2 paper

36. 1856. Coventry Ribbon Weavers' Association.

NOTICE.

MESSRS. J. T. & W. SMITH

HAVE THIS DAY AGREED TO PAY

THE LIST PRICE

For all WARPS given out in future.

D. BUTLER,

Secretary to the Coventry Ribbon Weavers' Association.

August 20th, 1858.

37. 1858. Coventry Ribbon Weavers' Association.

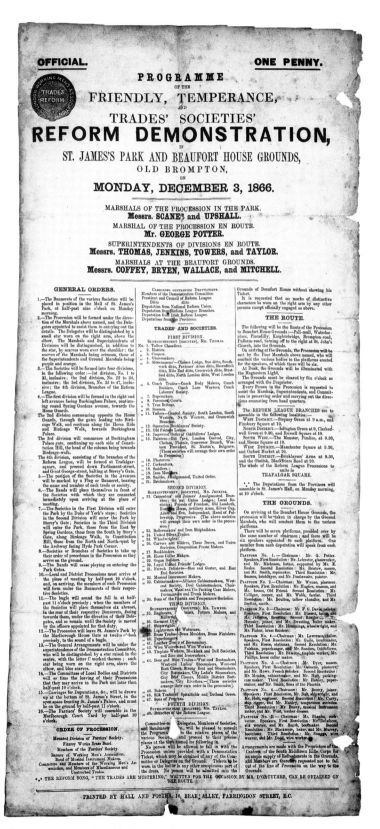

38. 1866. London Working Men's Association.

GAWCOTT LABOURERS.

We, a few Working Men, desire to lay before a discerning Public the following facts.—We are poor men, and wish to have facts fairly stated, as the only thing that can give us a standing in the sight of the Public.

For a *long time* we have *complained* and stated our position to our Employers. In some cases we have been laughed at, and had indefinite promises. We would have them remember "Whoso mocketh the poor reproacheth his Maker." We have worked all winter at nine and ten shillings per week; we are willing to take the sum of twelve shillings per week; (these last few weeks some have had eleven shillings,) other places they have had twelve all winter. To show that the former price was not enough,

J. C. has a wife and eight children; one boy earns three shillings per week.
W. M. has a wife and five children.
E. E. has a wife and four children.
W. S. has a wife and three children.

This is a sample of some of the families who have lived, or rather had an existence, by this ten shillings per week. What is a man to spend when he has paid

Rent, 1s. 6d.   Firing, 1s. 0d.   Bread, at 7½d per loaf.

We leave these facts with you and your families. We have nothing for the Clothier, Draper, Butcher, and Shoemaker, &c. Where are we Labourers with our industry? why on the verge of pauperism.

The men we work for, some have grown well to do within our recollection.

We are sober men—Home loving men—Wish to be honest men—We have cried unto our God, and we trust he has heard us—We appeal to you fathers of families, for sympathy—There is enough for all of us in this land—We appeal to you christian men—We appeal to you Ministers of religion, you who preach to us and tell us, in the House of God to say "Our Father," and tell us he is your "Father," and my "Father," and all ye are "Brethren." "The rich and the poor meet together, and the Lord is the Maker of them all." "Thou shalt not (starve) kill." We ask you to stand forth, and preach against oppression, tyranny, and for universal brotherhood from the pulpit, and come down with us to the stern *realities of life*. We ask that we may live, not as paupers, but by our own industry. We are willing to work, in order that our families may live. All we now ask is twelve shillings per week, and those who work on Sundays, one shilling more. For this application, some of us had part of our week's wages put into our hands, and dismissed there and then. Will this advance of one shilling bring ruin upon our Employers? We know it will not, but it will enable us to have more to eat, in order for us to do our work to their satisfaction.

Your friend,

Edward Easter, for Gawcott Labourers.

Mr. Thomas Baker, junior, has kindly consented to be our Treasurer.

March 11th, 1867.

39. 1867. Gawcott Labourers.

"THE NORTHERN DAILY EXPRESS,"
AND ITS
LATE STAFF OF COMPOSITORS.

The Compositors lately employed at the *Northern Daily Express* office, Newcastle, desire to publish a brief statement of the circumstances which have led to their being locked out. They do so in order to put themselves right with those who are taking an interest in the matter, and to rebut the calumny attempted to be cast upon them by Mr. Simpson, the local manager.

Since the *Express* last changed owners, and became the property of the present proprietary, alterations have been continually made, to the annoyance and injury of every department in the office. This has been done notwithstanding the arguments which Mr. Saunders, one of the proprietors, volunteered, in a speech delivered when the paper passed into their hands, to the effect that Printers, as a class, would not be injured by the system of stereotyping, enabling them to supply a number of newspapers with *the same leading articles* and summary of news! Men's real principles, however, can in some cases be more accurately discerned from their acts than from their words.

Although aware that the Compositors in the office were members of the Printers' Union, and bound by its laws, the Manager recently introduced one apprentice more than the recognised number. In order to conciliate, and avoid unpleasantness, the men, after consultation, conceded this point; but no sooner had they done so, than they were told that they must leave the Union, and allow still more lads to enter the office as apprentices. With these demands the men could not comply, and they were dismissed with a fortnight's notice. Hence the state of idleness in which they have been compelled to pass the last fortnight.

In the *Newcastle Daily Journal* of May 5th, Mr. Simpson states that it was not " made a condition of their remaining that they leave the Union until after they got their discharge." We most emphatically state that it was. The apprentice question had been settled, and the men thanked for making the concession. " Unfortunately," says Mr. Simpson, " the present is not the only dispute that has occurred during the past year. Some months ago, in changing from day wages to piece prices, the men were offered a rate by which they *would make higher wages than they actually accepted!*" This is something new for working men to learn. Whoever heard of a body of men refusing to have their wages advanced? The truth is, the proprietors proposed a very complicated scale of prices, offering a trifle extra for bad manuscript, &c., (but they were to be the sole judges of what was good and bad writing,) for which the men were to be deprived of all leaded matter, or, in other words, they were to be deducted so many lines whenever they happened to have a fair share of " fat." This, it will be obvious, was certain to lead to endless disputes, and we therefore declined to accept such one-sided terms, preferring the scale adopted by the other two daily newspaper offices, and which have been paid for a number of years.

But if anything were wanting to show the real object of the proprietors of the *Express*, it is seen in their act of reducing the price of composing **100** lines from 3s. 2d. to 2s. 10d. This reduction was effected on the earnings of the new hands who succeeded us for two weeks, and the proper price is only now paid through fear of losing more hands, three of the recently-engaged having left in disgust at the advantage taken of them.

It is obvious that the proprietors of the *Northern Daily Express* insist upon their Compositors being unconnected with a Trade Society, that they may be able to take every mean advantage, and not only reduce the remuneration of labour paid by other honourable employers in the town, but introduce an unlimited number of apprentices into a trade already overcrowded, one-fourth of the Compositors of England being almost constantly unemployed, such unemployed being maintained by a self-imposed tax paid by those in work. Thus, whilst the proprietors of the " Northern Daily Express" advocate freedom and free trade, their actions belie their professions : like the boastful teetotaller, who proclaims at Exeter Hall a donation of a thousand guineas, and then resorts to a thousand meannesses to extort the amount from the hard earnings of his Compositors. Will the enlightened public of Newcastle-on-Tyne lend their support and countenance to such oppressive tyranny, and such unfair competition ?

Newcastle-on-Tyne, May 20th, 1868.

40. 1868. Newcastle Typographical Association.

LONDON TRADES' COUNCIL.

REPEAL OF THE CRIMINAL LAW AMENDMENT ACT.

TO TRADE SOCIETIES,
AND ALL ORGANIZED BODIES OF WORKMEN.

LONDON
TRADES' DEMONSTRATION
Whit-Monday, June 2nd, 1873.

ADDRESS.

In calling upon the Trades of London to join in the forthcoming Demonstration, we have to remind them that both the Trades' Union Congresses, held in Nottingham and Leeds, declared decisively for nothing short of the repeal of the "Criminal Law Amendment Act," and such alteration in the "Master and Servants' Act," and "Law of Conspiracy," as shall secure precisely the same freedom of action, with justice and equality before the Law, for Workmen as for Employers. The collective opinion of the Unionists, as expressed in clear and definite resolutions at the Congresses referred to, was followed up last year by great Demonstrations of the Trades in most of the large Towns of England; but London in this respect has been silent. It is now time, however, for the Workmen to speak plainly and emphatically on the subject of Class Legislation, and to follow it up by the necessary action for its removal.

This course is now rendered more than ever imperative. Already the attitude of the Employers is both ominous and threatening. Two meetings have just been held, one in London, the other in Manchester, representing powerful and wealthy organizations of Employers, with the avowed object of opposing Mr. Vernon Harcourt in the effort he is about to make in Parliament to effect the just alteration in the Law which we desire.

These circumstances induced the London Trades' Council to convene a Delegate Meeting, at which it was decided to hold a Great Demonstration in Hyde Park, on Whit-Monday, June 2nd, and the following Societies were represented:—

"Tin-plate Workers, General Union Basket Makers, Amalgamated Engineers, Amalgamated House Decorators and Painters, Gas-Meter Makers, Cocoa Fibre Mat and Matting Makers, London Central Decorators and Painters, Zinc Workers, Tanners Unity, Grosvenor Society of Painters, London Consolidated Bookbinders, Postal and Telegraph Service Association, London Division Basket Makers, Metropolitan Operative Plasterers, Lambeth Society Basket Makers, United Order of Smiths', Co-operative Tin-plate Workers, Hand-in-Hand Gilders, London Operative Bricklayers, Gold Beaters, London and Westminster Bookbinders, Amalgamated Metal Workers, Alliance Cabinet Makers, Consolidated Bookbinders and Machine Rulers, Tobacco Pipe Makers, St. Martin's Painters' Society, City Boot Makers, Skinners, Amalgamated Turners, Saddle and Harness Makers, Deal Cabinet Makers, West-End Boot Closers, Wire Weavers, West-End Ladies' Boot and Shoe Makers, Union Gilders' Society, Amalgamated Labourers' Union, West-End Cabinet Makers, Friends of Freedom Carpenters and Joiners, Amalgamated Tailors' Society, Seamens' Association, General Alliance of Painters, City Womens' Shoe Makers, Gardeners' Association, London Paviors' Society" and many other Trades that have not yet held their special meetings on the subject.

Each Society must seriously consider its duty in this matter, and recognise the necessity of taking an active part in the intended Demonstration; as it must have not only the advantage of protesting against the present state of Class Legislation affecting working men, but will display the usefulness and power of organization to non-society men, and induce them to become members of those bodies who are working for their common protection and benefit.

Every working-man should remember that the power of the Law is precisely the same as when the Magistrate at Hammersmith Police Court sentenced an Engineer to two months imprisonment, for simply distributing hand-bills, informing men that a contest was pending between some workmen and their employers, and although an appeal was made against the sentence, we would call attention to the "note" on the case, issued in a report by the Parliamentary Committee last year as follows:—" We have since learned that the young man, John Turk, had to suffer all the indignities of an ordinary criminal, for three days, previous to being bailed out. His hair was cropped after the true felon type, and for three days he worked on the tread-mill as a common felon. And this is the law which Masters' Associations wish to perpetuate and enforce."

It is simple, therefore, the duty of every section of working-men to take immediate action to make the Demonstration as imposing as possible, and show their determination to have equality for workmen before the Law, and only complain when they feel the lash of its injustice. Remember now is the hour to act, and do not have to reflect that when duty called you were absent.

PRELIMINARY PROGRAMME.

The following Preliminary Programme was agreed upon, at a Meeting of the Trades' Delegates, held on Tuesday Evening, the 6th of May.

1. THAT the Demonstration take place on Whit-Monday, June 2nd, to consist of a Procession of the Trades, and a Meeting in Hyde Park.

2. That the place of Meeting for marshalling the Procession to be VICTORIA THAMES EMBANKMENT, the head of the Procession to be formed facing the Clock Tower of the Houses of Parliament, and extending down the Embankment towards Blackfriars Bridge.

3. That all Trade Societies, or Organized Bodies of Workmen, taking part in the Demonstration, be at their appointed stations on the Embankment (which will be duly notified to them by the organization committee) punctually at 12 o'clock, leaving the Embankment for Hyde Park precisely at 1 o'clock.

4. That the head of the Procession be formed of the London Trades' Council, the Demonstration Committee, and the Deputations from the Provincial Trades and Trades' Councils.

5. The Trades to follow in Sections, each branch of Trade or manufacture to form a section, viz.: the Iron Trades (to include, for example, the Engineers, Boiler-makers, Ironfounders, Smiths, Brass and Metal Workers, &c.); the Building Trades, the Clothing Trades, the Printing, Bookbinding and Paper Trades, the Leather Trades, the Cabinet-making, and Fancy Goods Trades, the Tin and Metal Trades, the Shipping and Ship-building Trades, the Silver and Jewellery Trades, the Coach and Carriage Trades, Miscellaneous and Small Trades, Organized Bodies of Workmen. The order of the Trades in each Section, and the order of the Sections in the Procession, to be arranged by ballot.

6. That each Section be preceded by a Banneret, with the number of the Section, and the names of the Trades comprising it, and that each Section be provided with a Band at its head, at the expense of the general fund. That every trade be accompanied by its trade banners and emblems.

7. That no party political banners, or mottoes, be on any account allowed in any part of the Procession.

8. The Route from the Embankment to Hyde Park to be as follows:—Parliament Street, Charing Cross, Cockspur Street, Pall Mall, Waterloo Place, Regent Street, Piccadilly Circus, Regent Street, Oxford Street, entering the Park by the Marble Arch. The Meeting in the Park to commence as near 3 o'clock as possible.

9. That all Non-Society-men, desirous of taking part in the Procession, are requested to fall in with the Society representing the Trade to which they belong.

10. That every person taking part in the Procession or Demonstration, be requested to provide himself, before the day, with an Official Demonstration Card, to be obtained of the Committee, or Delegates, at One Penny each.

Notice to Trade Societies, &c.

The Organization Committee, for carrying out the details connected with the Demonstration, sits daily at the "BELL INN," Old Bailey, from 10 a.m., until 9, p.m., where Bills, Programmes, Demonstration Cards (one penny each), and every information can be obtained.

At the Delegate Meetings the following, amongst other resolutions have been adopted:—

"That the Trades' Congress Parliamentary Committee, and Friendly, Temperance, Co-operative, and Organized Bodies of Workmen, with Deputations from the Provincial Trades and Trades' Councils, be invited to take part in the Demonstration."

"That all Societies be requested to call at once Special Meetings of their respective bodies, and appoint a committee to arrange all internal matters connected with themselves, and Delegates to represent them on the General Committee, held every Tuesday Evening, at 8 o'clock, at the "BELL INN," Old Bailey."

"That any Society intending to provide its own Band, be requested to communicate such information to the Organizing Committee immediately."

Further arrangements will be duly reported in future Circulars.

On behalf of the Organizing Committee,

GEORGE SHIPTON, Secretary.

COMMITTEE ROOM, "BELL INN," OLD BAILEY—MAY 7, 1873.

41. 1873. London Trades' Council.

LABOUR REPRESENTATION.

GREAT DEMONSTRATION

AT ROCHDALE,
ON SATURDAY, APRIL 18th, 1874.

Programme of the Day's Proceedings, Commencing at 2·30, p.m.

The Trades taking part in the Procession will commence to assemble, as early as possible, at the West end of the Town Hall and into Manchester-road, according to the order in which they have been balloted. Each Trade must nominate a Marshal, to act under the direction of the Chief Marshal. Each Trade Marshal will be distinguished by a White Rosette. Boards, with the number of each trade painted conspicuously, will be placed, so that every person on his arrival may have no difficulty in finding the Trade to which he belongs. It is requested that the Deputations from Oldham, Bury, and visitors from a distance fall in with their respective Trades.

Order of Procession.

CHIEF MARSHALS
ON HORSEBACK.
Chairman, Treasurer, Secretaries, and General Committee of the Demonstration (four abreast).

NORDEN BAND.
1. Miners of the District, accompanied by
TWO BANDS.

HIGH CROMPTON BRASS BAND.
2. Masons' Society.

SHAW CHURCH INSTITUTE BAND.
3. Amalgamated Engineers.

BAND.
4. Painters' Society,

5. Woollen Trades.

6. Iron Founders.

7. Silk Trades.

8. Warpers.

9. Beamers, Twisters, and Drawers.

10. Miscellaneous Trades.

11. Smiths' Benevolent Society.

Band of the 24th L.R.V.
12. Self-acting Minders.

13. Cabinet and Chair Makers.

14. Joiners.

15 Coach Builders.

16. Shoeing Smiths.

ROUTE OF PROCESSION.

Drake-street, Milnrow-road, Molesworth-street, John-street, Yorkshire-street, Regent-street, Taylor-street, Whitworth-road, Yorkshire-street, Cheetham-street, St. Mary's Gate, Blackwater-street, Lord-street, Manchester-road (fifty yards beyond Mr. Ashworth's House; Sparth Field); returning down Manchester-road to the Town Hall,

Immediately the last of the Procession reaches the Town Hall,

THE OPEN AIR MEETING

Will commence, the Chair to be taken by a WORKING-MAN.

THE FOLLOWING RESOLUTIONS WILL THEN BE MOVED.

1. "That this meeting of the Workingmen, connected with the staple industries of Rochdale and surrounding Towns, hereby expresses its great satisfaction that the direct representation of Labour in the House of Commons is now an accomplished fact, by the return of Messrs. Macdonald and Burt for Stafford and Morpeth respectively."

2. "That this meeting of Workingmen, connected with the two sections of political parties of this country, hereby expresses its full confidence in Messrs. Macdonald and Burt as the exponents of the thoughts, wishes, and sentiments, of the Working Community of this country."

THE EVENING MEETING

At Half-past Seven, presided over by JAMES ASHWORTH, Esq., Sparthfield, Rochdale.

THE FOLLOWING RESOLUTIONS WILL THEN BE MOVED.

1. "That we, the Burgesses of Rochdale, in public Meeting assembled, most heartily congratulate Messrs. Macdonald and Burt on their return as members of the new Parliament, and trusts that their presence in the National Legislature will conduce to more cordial relations between the various sections of the community of this country."

2. "That whilst reserving our own individual opinions respecting the policy of the present Government in issuing a Royal Comission to enquire into the laws affecting Labour, this meeting most cordially approves of the action of Mr. Macdonald in accepting a seat on that Commission at the last moment."

3. "That this meeting hereby tenders its hearty thanks to the electors of Stafford and Morpeth respectively as the first constituencies in the United Kingdom to recognize the rights of Labour to Parliamentary representation, by electing Workingmen to seats in the present House of Commons."

Tea will be provided at the Public Hall, at Five o'clock, Tickets 1s. 3d. each,

Tickets may be had at the Waggons in Front of the Town Hall, or at Messrs. SCHOFIELD & HOBLYN'S, Printers, Drake Street, Rochdale.

42. 1874. Labour Representation League.

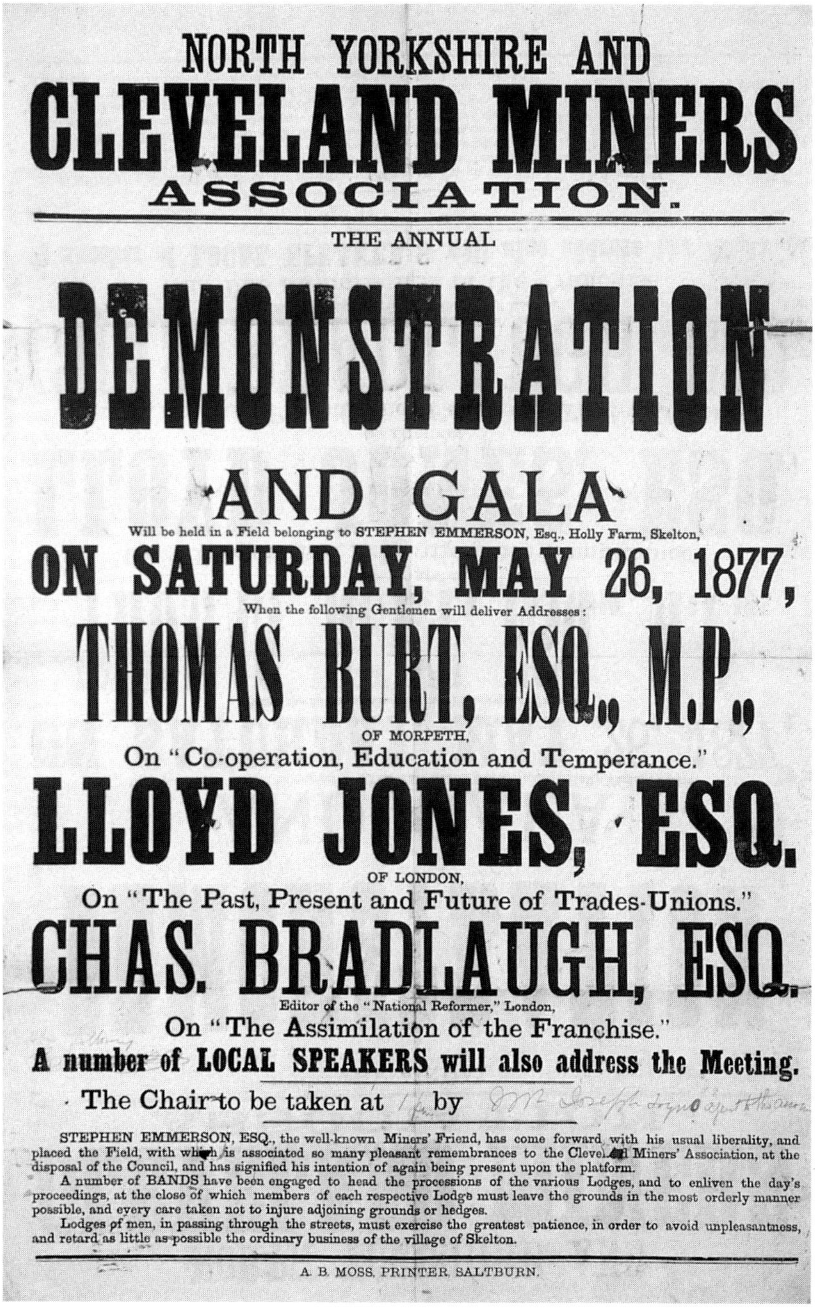

NORTH YORKSHIRE AND
CLEVELAND MINERS
ASSOCIATION.

THE ANNUAL

DEMONSTRATION

AND GALA

Will be held in a Field belonging to STEPHEN EMMERSON, Esq., Holly Farm, Skelton,

ON SATURDAY, MAY 26, 1877,

When the following Gentlemen will deliver Addresses:

THOMAS BURT, ESQ., M.P.,

OF MORPETH,

On "Co-operation, Education and Temperance."

LLOYD JONES, ESQ.

OF LONDON,

On "The Past, Present and Future of Trades-Unions."

CHAS. BRADLAUGH, ESQ.

Editor of the "National Reformer," London,

On "The Assimilation of the Franchise."

A number of LOCAL SPEAKERS will also address the Meeting.

The Chair to be taken at by

STEPHEN EMMERSON, ESQ., the well-known Miners' Friend, has come forward with his usual liberality, and placed the Field, with which is associated so many pleasant remembrances to the Cleveland Miners' Association, at the disposal of the Council, and has signified his intention of again being present upon the platform.

A number of BANDS have been engaged to head the processions of the various Lodges, and to enliven the day's proceedings, at the close of which members of each respective Lodge must leave the grounds in the most orderly manner possible, and every care taken not to injure adjoining grounds or hedges.

Lodges of men, in passing through the streets, must exercise the greatest patience, in order to avoid unpleasantness, and retard as little as possible the ordinary business of the village of Skelton.

A. B. MOSS, PRINTER, SALTBURN.

43. 1877. North Yorkshire and Cleveland Miners' Association.

NOTICE TO THE PUBLIC.

It being reported in various quarters that we, the **COMMITTEE** and **AGENTS** of the **MINERS' SOCIETY**, do acquiesce in the **CONDUCT, VIOLENCE** and **INTIMIDATION** now being used by certain parties terming themselves **COLLIERS**.

We beg leave to inform the **PUBLIC** at large, that we, the **COMMITTEE** and **AGENTS**, disclaim all such **CONDUCT, VIOLENCE** and **INTIMIDATION** on our part.

And further, that we **CONDEMN** all such **CONDUCT, VIOLENCE** and **INTIMIDATION**, as we think it detrimental to the interests of society at large, and us as well, and we neither do nor will recognise any Party or Parties using any such Conduct, Violence and Intimidation.

By order of the COMMITTEE and AGENTS.

P.S.-We respectfully request all men to refrain from attending such assemblies.

STROWGER, PRINTER, SCHOLES, WIGAN.

44. n.d. Wigan Miners' Association.

NOTICE TO THE PUBLIC

Some party or parties having placarded the walls of the Tow[n] with an anonymous placard, respecting the Miners' Society, we beg [to] inform the public, that any such bills will not be taken any notice of b[y] the Members of our Society, as they feel confident that our Officers a[nd] Agents are as much worthy of their office as any such men as kee[p] trying to delude the public with the state of affairs respecting us; a[nd] we beg further to inform the public, that some anonymous perso[ns] seem bent upon continuing their libellous conduct so long as our stri[ke] continues. If they be such men as they seem to be, why do they n[ot] state *facts*, and not *falsehoods*, and show the public where the[ir] placards are published as well as their names? It seems that suc[h] persons as sign themselves " *Your Well Wishers*," think that if t[he] ballot could be the arbitrator the strike would be at an end. Then w[as] not such person or persons have spoken about it at the public meeti[ng] in the Boys' Well Fields, when they had an opportunity, and not ke[ep] coming out in such anonymous ways and trying to make the publ[ic] believe we are almost idiots? It seems that such anonymous perso[ns] would like to get hold of one of our Quarterly Reports, as they seem t[o] think we have none, and if they would use it in a proper manner, ther[e] is no doubt but any member of the society would allow them to exami[ne] one; but before such persons get hold of one of our Reports, we hav[e] no hesitation in saying, they will have to come out in a more hon[est] way than what they have done.

Now, before we conclude, we must say a word or two about our so called " Boasted Unio[n]" If such persons had been in the society they would have no need to ask the public " Why are [the] Balance Sheets provided as is customary with other societies," they would have known witho[ut] asking the public, as they could see one at any time by applying at their Lodge. Now as to the ra[te] of wages paid in our district, we can prove to the public that there are men in other districts gett[ing] more money than what we are, and some making two or three hours a day less time; and furth[er] those anonymous persons wish to know where the amount of money has gone to, making [the] difference between the income and expenditure from the commencement of the Society up to [the] present time. We have no hesitation in saying that they would have known it had they been in th[e] Society. Then as to some of the Committee Men living in clover--those anonymous persons say the[y] have no difficulty in perceiving that " Some of the Committee Men are Living in Clover." If so, wh[y] not name those persons and expose them to the public in a proper manner? Then as to ou[r] Worth[y] Mayor examining some of the Masters' Pay Sheets, if they think some worthy of examin[ati]on wh[y] not all of them be examined? Then as to " Twenty or Thirty men being taken indiscriminatel[y] from those now on strike, and their opinions taken separately, they feel convinced that nine out [of] every ten would advocate working at the proposed reduction." If such be the case, why did not th[e] men say so at the Public Meeting, in the Boys' Well Fields, when the vote was put to them? Then a[s] to the so called " *Well Wishers*,"--" Hoping this may lead Colliers to a reasonable state of mind, an[d] put an end to this " DEPLORABLE STRIKE," we have no hesitation in saying that they are n[ot] " Well Wishers" of ours or they would not use such inflammatory language as they have done.

By Order of the Miners' Society.

PETER LIVSEY, Secretary.

STROWGER, PRINTER, WIGAN.

45. n.d. Wigan Miners' Association.

NATIONAL AGRICULTURAL
LABOURERS' UNION
BENEVOLENT FUND.

SUNDAY
SERVICES

IN CONNECTION WITH THE ABOVE, WILL BE HELD AT

Open air   Kelvedon

On SUNDAY, *next at 3. P.m.*

When SERMON**S** will be preached by

Mr. *Joseph Arch*

After which Collections will be made on behalf
of the above Fund, which assists a number of
aged men in time of Sickness, when too old
to join any Friendly Society. The kind help of
friends is asked for this worthy object.

" Inasmuch as ye have done it unto them, ye have done it unto Me."

CURTIS & BEAMISH, PRINTERS, LEAMINGTON.

Sankey's Hymns.

46. n.d. National Agricultural Labourers' Union.

Mass unionism and the First World War

The 1880s saw Britain still in the grip of the 'Great Depression' that had started in the previous decade. Foreign competition from Germany and the United States was pushing Britain off the top of the list of the world's foremost trading nations and the trade unions were beginning to feel the effects. Factory owners everywhere were investing in more, better and faster machines in an attempt to maintain profits, reduce labour costs and keep up with the competition. The new machines were changing the workforce by reducing the differentials between the skilled and the semi-skilled, something the older craft unions strongly resisted. Levels of unemployment and homelessness rose steeply and when the call went out to shorten the working day to eight hours so as to better share out the work that was available the older unions resisted again.

In his famous 1886 pamphlet *What a Compulsory Eight-Hour Working Day Means to the Worker* the thirty-year-old London engineer Tom Mann openly challenged the complacency of the old unions when he wrote:

> To Trade Unionists, I desire to make a special appeal. How long, *how long* will you be content with the present half-hearted policy of your unions? I readily grant that good work has been done in the past by unions, but in Heaven's name, what good purpose are they serving now? All of them have large numbers out of employment even when their particular trade is busy. None of the important societies have any policy other than of endeavouring to keep wages from falling. The true unionist policy of *aggression* seems entirely lost sight of; in fact the average unionist of today is a man with a fossilised intellect, either hopelessly apathetic, or supporting a policy that plays directly into the hands of the capitalist exploiters.

The pamphlet lit a spark that was to illuminate the work of many of the new general unions over the next few years for as one union member told the 1890 TUC conference, 'Those who accept the eight hour day are the new trade unionists, and those who do not are old unionists.'

It was not long before the increasing numbers of unemployed and homeless people began to make their presence felt on the streets of the big towns and cities. Up until the 1880s the middle classes and many better-off workers hardly noticed or even cared much about the plight of this growing army; it was only when visibly poor people began appearing in increasing numbers on the streets of central London in the winter of 1885/6 that the middle classes were forced to acknowledge the problem. Neither were they very concerned about the small political parties, like the Marx inspired Social Democratic Federation (SDF), that was beginning to organise. But this quickly changed when in February 1886 a large group of the unemployed rampaged round the West End after attending an SDF demonstration in Trafalgar Square. The arrest of some SDF leaders for sedition hit the headlines and fear of the mob returning the next day put the whole city on alert for months. No mob materialised but the unemployed and the homeless continued to roam the streets and sleep out in parks and shop doorways much to the disgust of the government and its middle-class supporters. Eighteen months later another and even larger demonstration was planned to take place in Trafalgar Square on Sunday 13 November; it was banned by the police which led to rioting and many arrests as thousands attempted to break the police and army cordons. 'Bloody Sunday', along with socialist and Marxist ideas much current at the time, did much to politicise many men and women who were later to become leading lights in the trade union movement, the Independent Labour Party and the Labour Party.

Trafalgar Square was an emblem of Britain's military prowess and trade unionism had now made its presence felt there. The next theatre of engagement between unions and the establishment was to be the London Docks, three miles to the east and a symbol of Britain's trading strength. Although still winning wars against local populations in Africa and elsewhere, Britain was continuing to lose the international trade war, and the dock companies and the thousands of workers in their employ were beginning to feel the pinch. In an attempt to maintain wage levels the dock workers went on strike and after receiving widespread support from many other unionists their demands were met. However, within a few years the employers clawed back their losses and used blacklegs in an attempt to break the unions.

All was not lost for the trade union movement as a whole emerged from the struggles of the last two decades of the nineteenth century both better organised, larger and – as a direct result of the dock strike – with two major new unions who organised 'general workers'; they later became the Transport & General Workers' Union and the General and Municipal Workers' Union. By 1900 the trade union movement had about 2 million members and despite the emergence of general unionism among the unskilled and semi-skilled it was in the older craft unions that most of the growth had occurred.

Women workers, like the match-girls at Bryant and May in 1888, did form their own organisations but women were still a small minority in the trade union movement as a whole. At the TUC Congress in 1888 a woman delegate moved a resolution 'that in the opinion of this Congress it is desirable, in the interests of both men and women, that in trades where women do the same work as men, they shall receive the same payment': this was hardly welcome in a movement that was institutionally opposed to women being in the workplace at all. Almost twenty years later one of the leaders of the 1889 London gas workers' strike said, 'Women do not make good trade unionists and for that reason we believe our energies are better used towards the organisation of male workers.' Even where women did organise, as in the National Federation of Women Workers founded in 1906, it was the middle classes that took the lead. There was a widespread belief that a woman's role was primarily that of being a bearer of children for the good of the 'British Race' and that any work outside the home would only distract her from this all-important task. And besides (men said) working women tended to lower wages. In many of the new clerical industries like the civil service, local government and education, where women did find employment, a marriage bar forced many to leave work on getting wed or to conceal their marriages altogether – a state of affairs that most unions, despite the successes of the suffrage movement, were not to challenge for decades to come.

Despite the 1876 Trade Union Act and a host of other legislation the legal position of trade unions was far from certain as they entered the new century. Government and the courts still dealt with unions under sufferance and many employers stubbornly refused to recognise unions at all. It was this lack of recognition that lay at the heart of the notorious Taff Vale case when, in 1900, a railway company successfully sued the railway workers' union for damages after it struck for recognition. The decision was overturned at appeal but then reversed by the House of Lords leaving the railway workers' funds open to legal claims. The Taff Vale judgment sent a shock wave through the trade union movement and in the run-up to the 1906 general election the TUC, the Labour Representation Committee and many trade unions publicly endorsed candidates whose platform include reversing the Taff Vale judgment.

The 1906 general election routed the Conservatives and brought into Parliament fifty-four Labour and Lib-Lab MPs of whom nine were members of the Parliamentary Committee of the TUC and twenty-nine were sponsored by the Labour Representation Committee, which now turned itself into the Labour Party. In the same year the Trades Dispute Act was passed giving unions back the immunity they had enjoyed before the Taff Vale judgment. However, the unions were not out of the woods yet for two years later the House of Lords ruled in the infamous Osborne case that there was no provision under the 1876 Act for unions to support their MPs via a political levy – the only means of subsistence for many of the new Labour MPs because they were still not salaried by the state. It took five years for the Osborne Judgment to be partially reversed by the 1913 Trade Union Act and for the State to agree to pay all MPs – something that the Chartists had campaigned for seventy years earlier.

In early August 1914 the trade union movement urged the government to 'decline to engage in war' and to confine its 'efforts to bringing about peace as soon as possible'. By the end of the month, after Germany had invaded Belgium on 4 August, much of the trade union movement and the Labour Party threw their combined weight behind the war effort and the TUC asked that there be an industrial truce for the duration. Two months later the now patriotic labour movement stayed completely silent when the oppressive Defence of Realm Act that curtailed free speech and street demonstrations was introduced.

Wartime conditions radically changed the relationship between the government and the trade unions. Patriotism became the driving force behind an unprecedented collaboration in which most unions agreed to sacrifice almost all of the gains they had built up over a century of persecution and strife in return for a say in government policy. Three union leaders were given seats in the cabinet and a further 2,000 or so unionists served on government advisory committees of one sort or another. As a *quid pro quo* the government agreed to the long-held TUC demand that there should be some public control of the mines, shipping and food distribution. However, these arrangements did not prevent unions from campaigning against war-profiteering or from pushing for better pay as profits in many industries rose well ahead of wages. With more than 5 million men – about one-third of the nation's male workforce – enlisted in the armed forces, the industrial position of those that remained behind strengthened, leading to the improvement in the position of many unskilled and semi-skilled workers. In some industries the craft unions resisted this 'dilution' and special arrangements had to be made to allow women into munitions production. Another outcome of the war was the growth of the shop stewards' movement which some believed would become a rank-and-file force that would eventually challenge the movement's leadership; in fact it petered out. Soon after the Armistice in 1918 the Labour Party pulled its ministers out of the government and the cosy arrangements that had developed during the war soon began to take on the chill of the pre-war days. The brief postwar boom created massive profits in many industries and workers struck for a larger slice of the cake: even the police in London joined in.

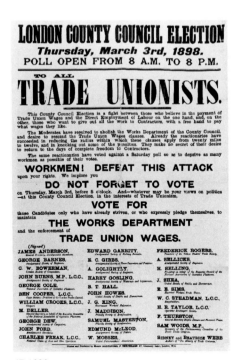

47. 1898.

The Posters 1880–1920

The posters in this section give some indication of the growth of general unionism, particularly in London, under the influence of socialist and European Marxist ideas and the eventual triumph of labour representation in Parliament.

(47) Soon after it was formed in 1889 the Progressive-dominated London County Council established a direct works department and imposed fair wage clauses on all suppliers of goods to the council. Through this policy the council built houses and other public buildings to high standards and improved pay rates in many London trades. When in power the Moderates and their successors, the Tories, generally opposed these arrangements right up until the abolition of the Greater London Council (GLC) in 1986.

(48, 58–60) Making provision for members in times of sickness and death had been an important part of most trade unions' work since their beginnings and social events to raise funds, including dances, concerts and tea parties accompanied by speeches from well-known figures in the movement, formed an important part of every trade union's calendar. They also often enabled women to mix in a usually male-dominated trade union world.

(49–51, 55) In the 1880s thousands of Jews escaping the pogroms of Poland and Russia sought safety and employment in London's East End. Many were skilled at tailoring or willing to learn but the conditions they found in the industry were appalling as ruthless employers exploited their need for work by paying rock-bottom wages and demanding long hours. By 1889 this 'sweating' system had become a national scandal and the government was forced to instigate an official inquiry but the tailors' unions were impatient and went on strike. The strike lasted five weeks and resulted in victory for the unions. Within weeks plans were set in train to bring together into a federation the many small unions in which Jews predominated but the idea came to nothing.

(52–4, 56) In early August 1889 the Tea Operatives' and General Labourers' Union working in London's West India Docks went on strike demanding an increase in their wages to sixpence an hour. Within days the 'Dockers' Tanner Strike' had spread across the whole of the docks bringing out stevedores, boilermakers, ballastmen, coal heavers and a host of general labourers. Through skilled organisation the dockers' leaders kept the strike in the public mind by daily marches, rallies and appeals for relief funds to help feed the workers and their families. Eventually the strike was settled on 12 September. The Tea Operatives' union grew from a membership of a 2,800 in 1888 to 57,000 in 1890 and renamed itself the Dock, Wharf, Riverside and General Labourers' Union. Successful as this union was it failed to organise workers on the south side of the river who formed themselves into a separate body titled the South Side Labour Protection League. Over the next twenty years the membership of these organisations declined and it was not until 1922 with the creation of Transport & General Workers' Union that the dock labourers became better organised.

(57) Sidney Shaftoe, Secretary of the Yorkshire United Skip and Basket Makers' Society, was a tireless campaigner for more 'labour' MPs in Parliament. In 1906 after fifty-four Labour and Lib-Lab MPs were elected to Parliament the previously named Labour Representation Committee became the Labour Party.

(61) In 1891 it was estimated that some 450,000 shop assistants 'lived in' with the employer paying them partly in cash and partly in kind by providing board and lodging. The system was open to widespread abuse and in 1901 thirteen shop assistants paraded down London's Oxford Street to draw attention to their plight. 'Living-in' continued until the 1920s when, after a long campaign by the Shop Assistants' Union, most workers gained the right to choose between taking board and being paid a full wage.

(62, 63) Disputes over the price paid by employers for the log (local piece price list) were common in the tailoring trades as here with the West End tailors and tailoresses.

(64) May Day celebrations became an important annual event for the labour and trade union movement after their inception by the Social Democratic Federation at a meeting in London's Hyde Park on 1 May 1894.

(65) Fifteen years after Joseph Arch's National Agricultural Labourers' Union dissolved, a new union, the National Agricultural Labourers' and Rural Workers' Union based in East Anglia, was formed. The new union endeavoured to organise carters, roadmen, gardeners, navvies and, for the first time, women. When it became the National Union of Agricultural Workers in 1920 it had 180,000 members.

(66) Women filled the teaching jobs left vacant by men during the First World War but had to fight for equal pay, a demand that most employers firmly resisted until after 1945.

48. 1883. United Tin-Plate Workers' Friendly and Protective Society of Glasgow and the West of Scotland.

TO TAILORS AND TAILORESSES ! ! !

GREAT STRIKE

of

LONDON TAILORS

& SWEATER'S VICTIMS.

FELLOW WORKERS,

You are all aware that a Commission of Lords have been appointed to enquire into the evils of the Sweating System in the Tailoring Trade. The Revelations made before the Commission by Witnesses engaged in the Tailoring Trade, are a Disgrace to a Civilized Country. The Sweaters' Victims had hoped that this Commission, would have come to some satisfactory conclusion as to an alteration in the condition of the Sweated Tailors. Finding they have just put off their deliberation until Next Session, we have decided to take Immediate Action.

It is too long for us to wait, until Next Session, because the hardships inflicted upon us by the Sweater are unbearable. We have therefore decided to join in the CENERAL DEMAND FOR INCREASED COMFORT AND SHORTER HOURS OF LABOUR. Our Hours at present being on an average from 14 to 18 per day, in unhealthy and dirty dens.

WE DEMAND:

(1) THAT THE HOURS BE REDUCED TO 12 WITH AN INTERVAL OF ONE HOUR FOR DINNER AND HALF-HOUR FOR TEA.

(2) ALL MEALS TO BE HAD OFF THE PREMISES.

(3) GOVERNMENT CONTRACTORS TO PAY WAGES AT TRADE UNION RATES.

(4) GOVERNMENT CONTRACTORS AND SWEATERS NOT TO GIVE WORK HOME AT NIGHT AFTER WORKING HOURS.

We now Appeal for the support of all Tailors to join us and thus enable us to Successfully Enforce our Demands, which are reasonable.

Tailors & Tailoresses support in joining this General Strike.

We Appeal to all Tailors, Machinists, Pressers, Basters, &c. to meet, EN-MASSE, on THURSDAY, FRIDAY & SATUR-DAY MORNINGS, at 10 o'clock, (outside the Baths) GOULSTON STREET, WHITECHAPEL, E.

Piece Workers Finish Up, Week Workers Give Notice at Once,

ALL WORK TO CEASE ON SATURDAY AFTERNOON WHEN THE STRIKE WILL BE DECLARED.

Signed, STRIKE COMMITTEE.

Lewis Lyons, Chairman	Richard Roskeliy,	Annie Goodman,	Jacob Sydler,	M. Rosenthall,
J. Green	Phillip White,	L. Goldstein,	J. Margolis,	Harris Frank
J. Silverman	Simon Cohen	Charles Mowbray,	D. Greenbaum	Lewis Perlburg,
				W. Wess, Secretary.

Tailors Strike Committee Room "White Hart," Greenfield st., Commercial-Rd. All communications to be addressed to the Secty

P.S. We appeal to those engaged in the Trade to at once join either of the following Societies:
"JEWISH BRANCH, AMALGAMATED SOCIETY OF TAILORS," Meets on Sunday Evenings, from 8 till 10, at the "White Hart," Greenfield Street, Commercial Road, E.
"PRESSER'S SOCIETY," Meet Sunday Evenings, from 8 till 10, at the "Man in the Moon," Plough Street, Commercial Road, E.
"MANTEL MAKERS, TAILORS AND MACHINISTS SOCIETY," Meet Saturday Evenings, from 7 till 10 at the "White Hart," Greenfield Street, Commercial Road, E.

AUGUST 27th, 1889

49. 1889. Amalgamated Society of Journeymen Tailors, Jewish Branch.

50. 1889. Amalgamated Society of Journeymen Tailors, Jewish Branch.

51. 1889. Amalgamated Society of Journeymen Tailors, Jewish Branch.

SOUTH SIDE
CENTRAL STRIKE COMMITTEE,
SAYES COURT, DEPTFORD.
SEPTEMBER 10, 1889.

GENERAL MANIFESTO.

Owing to the fact that the demands of the Corn Porters, Deal Porters, Granary Men, General Steam Navigation Men, Permanent Men and General Labourers on the South Side have been misrepresented, the above Committee have decided to issue this Manifesto, stating the demands of the various sections now on Strike, and pledge themselves to support each section in obtaining their demands.

DEAL PORTERS of the Surrey Commercial Docks have already placed their demands before the Directors.

LUMPERS (Outside) demand the following Rates, viz:— 1. 10d. per standard for Deals. 2. 11d. per stand. for all Goods rating from 2 x 4 to 2½ x 7, or for rough boards. 3. 1s. per std. for plain boards. Working day from 7 a.m. to 5 p.m., and that no man leave the "Red Lion" corner before 6.45 a.m. Overtime at the rate of 6d. per hour extra from 5 p.m. including meal times.

STEVEDORES (Inside) demand 8d. per hour from 7 a.m. to 5 p.m. 1s. per hour overtime. Overtime to commence from 5 p.m. to 7 a.m. Pay to commence from leaving "Red Lion" corner. Meal times to be paid for. Holidays & Meal times double pay, and that the Rules of the United Stevedores Protection League be acceded to in every particular. *Conceded*

OVERSIDE CORN PORTERS (S.C.D.) demand 15s.3d. per 100 qrs. for Oats. Heavy labour 17s.4d. per 100 qrs. manual, or with use of Steam 16s.1d. All overtime after 6 p.m. to be paid at the rate of ½d. per qr. extra.

QUAY CORN PORTERS (S. C. D.) demand the return of Standard prices previous to March 1889, which had been in operation for 17 years.

TRIMMERS AND GENERAL LABOURERS demand 6d. per hour from 7 a.m. to 6 p.m. and 8d. per hour Overtime; Meal times as usual; and not to be taken on for less than 4 hours.

WEIGHERS & WAREHOUSEMEN demand to be reinstated in their former positions without distinction.

BERMONDSEY AND ROTHERHITHE WALL CORN PORTERS demand:
1. Permanent Men 30s. per week. 2. Casual Men 5s. 10d. per day and 8d. per hour Overtime; Overtime to commence at 6 p.m. Meal times as usual.

GENERAL STEAM NAVIGATION MEN demand:—1. Wharf Men, 6d. per hour from 6 a.m. to 6 p.m. and 8d. per hour Overtime. 2. In the Stream, 7d. per hour ordinary time, 9d. per hour Overtime. 3. In the Dock, 8d. per hour ordinary time, 1s. per hour Overtime.

MAUDSLEY'S ENGINEER'S MEN. Those receiving 21s. per week now demand 24s., and those receiving 24s. per week demand 26s.

ASHBY'S, LTD., CEMENT WORKS demand 6d. per ton landing Coals and Chalk. General Labourers 10% rise of wages all round, this making up for a reduction made 3 years ago.

GENERAL LABOURERS, TELEGRAPH CONSTRUCTION demand 4s. per day from 6 a.m. to 5 p.m., time and a quarter for first 2 hours Overtime, and if later, time and a half for all Overtime. No work to be done in Meal Hours.

Signed on behalf of the Central Committee,
Wade Arms,
BEN. TILLETT,
JOHN BURNS,
TOM MANN,
H. H. CHAMPION,
JAS. TOOMEY.

Signed on behalf of the South side Committee,
JAS. SULLI...
CHAS. H...
HUGH J...

...side to be sent to Mr. HUGH BRO...   ...entral Strike Committee, Sayes Court,

52. 1889. South Side Central Strike Committee.

DOCK LABOURERS' STRIKE!
RELIEF FUND.

Fellow-workmen—An earnest appeal is made to you to help your fellow-workmen, the half-starved, under-paid Dockers, in their great struggle. The men MUST win, or so much the worse for all of us. It will be our fault if they do not. Their cause is the most righteous and reasonable in modern times.

GIVE LIBERALLY & SECURE THE VICTORY!

Public Relief Fund Sheets supplied to duly authorised Collectors. All Clubs and Institutions are asked to co-operate. Shops and Factories should appoint their own Collectors.

SUBSCRIPTIONS RECEIVED at the OFFICE OF COMMITTEE, 23, RUTLAND STREET, every Evening at 7.30 ; 4 on Saturday.

COMMITTEE-

John Potter, (Leicester School Board), Harry Woolley, (New Co-op. Shoe Works), Hipwell, (Vine St. Radical Club), C. O'Sullivan, (Irish Nationl Club), Messrs. L. Brown, Staughton, Warner, Gorrie, Barclay, Richards, &c.

53. 1889. Dock Labourers' Relief Fund, Leicester.

54. 1889. Dockers celebrate victory at the end of the 'Great Dock Strike'.

UNITY, FRATERNITY & STRENGTH!

Under the auspices of the

HEBREW CABINET MAKERS' SOCIETY, STICK AND CANE DRESSERS' UNION,
INTERNATIONAL FURRIERS' SOCIETY,
TAILOR-MACHINISTS' UNION, TAILORS' AND PRESSERS' UNION,
AMALGAMATED LASTERS' SOCIETY, UNITED CAPMAKERS' SOCIETY, AND
INTERNATIONAL JOURNEYMAN BOOT-FINISHERS' SOCIETY,

A

Mass Meeting

will take place on

SATURDAY, DECEMBER 28th, 1889,

at the

 GREAT ASSEMBLY HALL

MILE END ROAD, E.

To inaugurate the Federation of East-London Labour Unions.

The Chair will be taken at 3 p.m. prompt by

Mr. CHARLES V. ADAMS,

Who will be supported by the following speakers: Messrs.

**J. MACDONALD, TOM WALKER, J. TURNER,
TOM MANN, BEN TILLETT,
H. SPARLING, H. DAVIS, C. MOWBRAY,**
Mrs. SCHACK, WESS, WEINBERG, FEIGENBAUM,
ROCHMAN, M. FRENCHMAN, L. COHEN, LIGHTMAN,
SKITTEN, ROSENBERG, GOLDSTEIN, SEBERSKY,
LEEK, and GOLDSTONE.

All members of the above unions are earnestly requested to attend this
most important meeting.

WORKERS OF THE WORLD UNITE!

Communications in connection with the above to be addressed to the Hon. Sec.,
W. WESS, 12, Clark St. Bedford Sq. E.

א גרויסע

מאססע פּערזאמלונ

פֿעראנשטאלטעט פֿון אללע אידישע ארבּיטער פֿעראינען,

וועט שטאטפֿינדען

שבת, דעם 28-טען דעצעמבער, אום 3 אודר נאכמיטטאג, אין די

גרייט אסעמבלי האלל, מייל ענד ראוד

אום צו פֿייערן דיא גרינדונג פֿון דיא פֿעדעריישאן פֿון אללע ארבּיטער פֿעראי־

rker's Friend Printing Office, 40, Berner St., Commercial Rd. E.

55. 1889. Federation of East-London Labour Unions.

DOCK, WHARF, RIVERSIDE AND GENERAL LABOURERS' UNION

Of Great Britain and Ireland.

President: TOM MANN.   Treasurer: F. N. CHARRINGTON, L.C.C.   Gen. Sec.: BEN TILLETT.

Registered Office: 33, MILE END ROAD, E.

Our Motto: "A Nation Made free by love, a mighty Brotherhood Linked by a jealous interchange of good."

VICTORIA & ALBERT DOCK DISTRICT.

A MASS MEETING

WILL TAKE PLACE ON

Sunday, July 5th, 1891,

AT

MORLEY'S CORNER, BARKING ROAD,

AT 4 P.M.

When Addresses will be delivered by the following Friends of Labour, on the Benefits of Trades Unionism and Labour Representation:

PLATFORM No. 1.	PLATFORM No. 2.
CHAIRMAN:	CHAIRMAN:
BRO. TOM WATTS, D.L.U.	**COUNCILLOR GEO. LAMBERT**
SPEAKERS:	Labour Candidate North West Ham. D.L.U.
BEN TILLETT, JOHN BURNS,	SPEAKERS
D.L.U. L.C.C.	TOM MANN, J. H. WILSON,
TOM McCARTHY,	D.L.U. Gen.-Sec. Seamen and Firemen's Union.
D.L.U.	W. THORNE, DR. JOHN MOIR.
KEIR HARDIE, MR. RATCLIFF,	Gen.-Sec. Gas Workers' Union.
Labour Candidate South West Ham. Solicitor D.L.U.	

ON WHICH OCCASION THE

HANDSOME NEW SILK BANNER

Of the TIDAL BASIN No. 3 BRANCH will be unfurled by

JOHN BURNS and KEIR HARDIE.

A Grand Procession will start from the District Office, 225, Victoria Dock Road, at 2.30 p.m., and march through the principal Streets to Morley's Corner.

All Trade Unions are cordially invited.

COME IN YOUR THOUSANDS AND SUPPORT TRADE UNIONISM.

ALL SHOULD READ THE "TRADE UNIONIST."

W. KRANC, Branch Secretary.   H. STYLES, District Secretary.
TOM WATTS, Branch Chairman.   J. FAIRBAIRN, District Chairman.

GEO. REYNOLDS, 23,Stepney Green. London, E.

56. 1891. Dock, Wharf, Riverside and General Labourers' Union.

WORCESTER
LABOUR REPRESENTATIVE
ASSOCIATION.

THE ANNUAL

PUBLIC MEETING

WILL BE HELD AT THE

Co-Operative Hall,
ST. NICHOLAS STREET,

TUESDAY, SEPT. 26th, 1893,

WHEN

COUNCILLOR SHAFTOE, J.P.,

(Of BRADFORD,)

Ex-President of Trades Union Congress,

AND OTHERS, WILL SPEAK ON LABOUR REPRESENTATION.

⊀ THE CHAIR WILL BE TAKEN AT 8 P.M. ⊁

Electors and Ladies are Particularly Invited.

FORWARD LABOUR!!

57. 1893. Worcester Labour Representative Association.

58. 1893. National Amalgamated Sailors' and Firemen's Union of Great Britain and Ireland.

NATIONAL AMALGAMATED
Sailors & Firemen's Union.

THE FOURTH ANNUAL

TEA & BALL

IN AID OF THE

Widows & Orphans' Fund,

WILL BE HELD IN THE

FREE LIBRARY HALL,

SOUTH SHIELDS, ON

Wednesday, Dec. 20th.

1893

TEA on the TABLES at 5 p.m.   Councillor J. ABBOTT, M.C., will lead off the Dance at 8 p.m.

Tea & Ball 1/6 Double Tickets 2/6 Tea 1/- Ball 1/-

Owing to the great success last year, it is hoped that all friends will secure their tickets as early as possible to avoid any inconvenience.   Tickets can be had at the Hall, or from any of the Officials.

D. CLEMENT,
SECRETARY.

R. SIMPSON & SONS, PRINTERS, "FREE PRESS" OFFICE, CHAPTER ROW, SOUTH SHIELDS.

59. 1893. National Amalgamated Sailors' and Firemen's Union of Great Britain and Ireland.

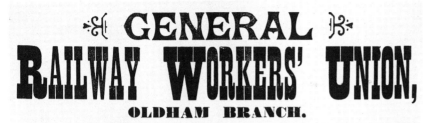

❈ GENERAL ❈
RAILWAY WORKERS' UNION,
OLDHAM BRANCH.

THE FIRST ANNUAL

TEA ❈ PARTY
AND
❈ CONCERT ❈

WILL BE HELD AT THE

CO-OPERATIVE HALL, KING STREET, OLDHAM.

ON SATURDAY, FEB. 28, 1891,

Under the Patronage of the following Gentlemen :--

J. BEDFORD, Esq., of London,
President of G. R. W. U.

W. A. GREAVES, Esq., A. BUCKLEY, Esq.,
Vice-President, Oldham Trades' Council.   Secretary, Weavers' Association.

THE FOLLOWING WELL-KNOWN ARTISTES WILL APPEAR:--

Miss Teresa Haynes, Miss Ada Pendlebury,
Soprano; of the Lancashire Concerts.   Contralto; of the English and Scotch Concerts.

Mr. S. R. WALKER, Mr. R. MEREDITH,
Tenor; of the Lancashire Concerts.   Baritone; late of Mr. Ben Lang's and Lancashire Concerts.

Mr. FRED OLIVER, Mr. S. MELLOR,
Humorist; of the Oldham and District Concerts.   Accompanist.

Tea on the Tables at 5 p.m., Concert to commence at 7-30.

CARRIAGES ORDERED FOR 10-30 P.M.

TICKETS:-Tea Party & Concert, 1s.; Concert only, 6d.;

May be had from the Committee, or any Members of the Branch.

G. H. LEES & Co., Printers and Stationers, 13, Lees Road, Oldham.

60. 1897. General Railway Workers' Union.

61. 1901. Shop assistants campaigning against the 'living-in' system prepare to march down London's Oxford Street.

THE LONDON SOCIETY OF TAILORS AND TAILORESSES.

16, HEDDON STREET, REGENT STREET, LONDON, W.

AN APPEAL

TO THE TAILORS & TAILORESSES OF LONDON.

" The Masters refuse to Accede to the New Regulations, calling them unjust, because, say they, the Men have Six Shillings per day, which Wages by the New Regulations would be increased Twenty-Five per cent."—Extract from an Address issued by the Journeymen Tailors of the Metropolis, May, 1834.

FELLOW WORKERS,—

Nearly a hundred years ago the Journeymen Tailors of London deemed SIX SHILLINGS A DAY an inadequate return for their services. How far have we advanced since then? How many would be glad to have that sum guaranteed to them for the forthcoming year's labour? How is it that, with the evidence of enormous wealth on every hand, the Journeyman Tailor of to-day is relatively to the journeyman of 1834 WORSE OFF? One might well ask what has the great increase of national wealth done for us? Our work has not deteriorated in skill, nor in the expenditure of physical energy required to do it. Collectively, the national comfort has increased during the past century by leaps and bounds; Tailors' wages have gone down, judged by their purchasing power. But even if wages had increased in equal ratio to the great increase in national wealth, what then? Are we enjoying a standard of living that satisfies the natural desires of man? Have we and our dependants at all times a sufficiency of domestic comfort? Are the conditions under which we work such as to secure us in the enjoyment of natural, healthy lives? You know they are not. Too well is it known to all, the HAUNTING FEAR of having a shortage in the week's earnings. THE DREAD OF NO LOG, and the constant fear of not being able to meet the week's liabilities, is constantly with us, slowly, but nevertheless surely, sapping away our strength and energy, until worn out not so much with actual hard work as with the never-ending, ceaseless anxiety of making ends meet.

Is it worth it? Is life worth living under the conditions it is carried on to-day? To the favoured few perhaps it is, but to the majority we say, No, it is not. To keep on living the lives that the great bulk of our craft live is a crime against the family, and a crime against their fellow workers, who are desirous of obtaining a better standard of living.

To say that better conditions cannot be obtained is nonsense; they can and will be obtained if desired. But to obtain them it needs the individuals to make up their minds that they wish for a change. The London Society has collectively determined to have a try to bring about better conditions for the trade; if they can enlist the same desire in the minds of the men and women of London, then success is assured.

They appeal not to the old fossil-minded, sit-at-home people, who are content to wallow in their misery so long as they are not disturbed, many of them young in years but old, old indeed in spirit. To the men and women desirous of breaking with the soul-destroying and body-devouring system of the present, the demand for your service is made; to you belongs the future of our industry, and with you belongs the right of determining whether an effort to better our working conditions is to be made or not.

A cry is being made as to the present division in the ranks of our industry. Don't be misled, there can be no division if the workers wish to better themselves; no other cry or object can unite us but the one, and that is one that will lead to the material benefit of the workers. Hence the banner raised to rally our forces is inscribed with the demands for — WORKSHOP ACCOMMODATION, REVISION OF THE LOG, AN INCREASE OF WAGES. If you are with us in these demands, report yourself at once to either of the Committee Rooms.

LIST OF COMMITTEE ROOMS AND MEMBERS OF CENTRAL COMMITTEE IN CHARGE.

(1) HAMMOND'S & TAUTZ & SHOPS WEST OF BOND STREET. —J. O'Neill, Three Compasses, Orchard Street.

(2) HILL'S AND ST. JAMES ST. SHOPS.—H. Svendsen, Swallow Rooms, Swallow Street.

(3) SHOPS SOUTH OF PICCADILLY TO HAYMARKET.— H. Lockwood, Queen's Head, Denman Street.

(4) SACKVILLE STREET AND REGENT STREET SHOPS, AND HAWKE'S.—C. Hepburn, Duke of Argyll.

(5) POOLE'S AND BLOCK ROUND BOND STREET.—A. Brass, Oriental Cafe, 30, Kingley Street.

(6) SANDEN'S SIDE OF SAVILE ROW AND NEW BURLINGTON STREET.—A. Hill, Tap House, Ingestre Place.

(7) CLIFFORD STREET (NORTH SIDE) ROUND CONDUIT STREET (SOUTH SIDE) TO BOND STREET.—A. Nowick, Burlington Arms.

(8) NORTH SIDE CONDUIT STREET AND SOUTH SIDE FROM MILL STREET TO REGENT STREET.—A. Kaufhald, Hungarian Restaurant, 26, Foubert's Place.

(9) MADDOX STREET AND GEORGE STREET, FROM CHURCH TO CONDUIT STREET.—R. George, Two Chairmen, 111, Wardour Street.

(10) HANOVER SQUARE & GEORGE STREET TO CHURCH.— T. Shine, Coach and Horses, Poland Street.

(11) HANOVER STREET AND PRINCE'S STREET.—A. Barron, Marlboro' Inn, Marlboro Mews.

(12) BROOK STREET AND SOUTH MOLTON STREET.— A. Burlin, Clarendon, 364, Oxford Street.

(13) GRAFTON ST., ALBEMARLE ST. & DOVER ST.—Levenyak, Glenton's, Bruton Mews.

Twentieth Century Press, Ltd. (Trade Union & Forty-Eight Hours), 37a, Clerkenwell Green, London, E.C. (7234)

62. 1909. London Society of Tailors and Tailoresses.

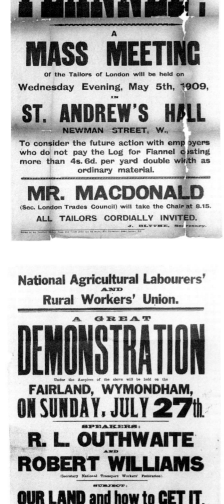

LONDON SOCIETY OF
TAILORS AND TAILORESSES
FLANNEL!
A
MASS MEETING
Of the Tailors of London will be held on
Wednesday Evening, May 5th, 1909,
IN
ST. ANDREW'S HALL
NEWMAN STREET, W.,
To consider the future action with employers who do not pay the Log for Flannel costing more than 4s. 6d. per yard double width as ordinary material.

MR. MACDONALD
(Sec. London Trades Council) will take the Chair at 8.15.
ALL TAILORS CORDIALLY INVITED.
J. BLYTHE, Secretary.

Brighton & District Trades & Labour Council.
LABOUR DAY
DEMONSTRATION
Sunday, May 4.
Procession leaving AQUARIUM at 3 o'clock, headed by the
Band of the Amalgamated Musicians' Union
Proceeding to
THE LEVEL,
where a
MASS MEETING
will be addressed by
Mr. A. BELLAMY, President, National Union of Railwaymen
Mr. T. LOWTH, Chief Organising Sec., N.U.R.
Mr. PERCY YOUNG, Gen. Sec., Hotel Workers' Union
Mr. G. ELMER, Organiser, United Builders' Labourers' Union
LOCAL and OTHER NATIONAL SPEAKERS.

ALL WORKERS MUST JOIN THE RANKS.
FOR ROUTE AND FURTHER PARTICULARS SEE HANDBILLS.

National Agricultural Labourers'
AND
Rural Workers' Union.
A GREAT
DEMONSTRATION
Under the Auspices of the above will be held on the
FAIRLAND, WYMONDHAM,
ON SUNDAY, JULY 27th.
SPEAKERS:
R. L. OUTHWAITE
AND
ROBERT WILLIAMS
(Secretary National Transport Workers' Federation).
SUBJECT:
OUR LAND and how to GET IT.
Chair to be taken at THREE p.m. by
E. G. GOOCH (President of the Wymondham Labour Party.)
Come in your thousands to hear Labour's Orators

63. 1909. London Society of Tailors and Tailoresses.
64. 1913. Brighton and District Trades and Labour Council.
65. 1919. National Agricultural Labourers' and Rural Workers' Union.

66. 1916. Women teachers in Buxton march for equal pay during the First World War.

Depression and the Second World War

The trade unions entered the 1920s in a militant mood as serious unemployment quickly followed the short postwar boom. As the economy began to decline and foreign competition intensified employers sought to reduce costs by cutting wages and laying off workers. The immediate postwar coalition government dominated by the Conservatives quickly shed any pretence of cooperation with the unions and dealt ruthlessly with strikes, fearing a revolutionary mood would spread from the newly established Soviet Union to the rank-and-file. However, cuts in wages and rising unemployment failed to restore British competitiveness and it soon became clear that the current policy was no way to national prosperity. Many trade unions resorted to industrial action in an attempt to stall the fall in pay. In fact 1920 and 1921 saw more disputes than any other year of the interwar period except 1926: this high level of activity was during a time when unemployment had reduced trade union membership by almost 20 per cent.

Alongside this rise in industrial action and fall in membership the TUC began to reorganise itself in order to operate more effectively under the new conditions. Faced with the formation of a series of employers' associations and several disputes that had failed because of a lack of united action by the trade unions, the TUC decided to replace its Parliamentary Committee with a General Council that would coordinate industrial action, influence inter-union disputes and enter into agreements with union movements in other countries. However, various unions objected that this General Council would limit their freedom to act as they saw fit and this resulted in the new body having greater responsibilities than the Parliamentary Committee but without the power to carry out them out. Despite this setback the General Council and the Labour Party Executive established joint departments for research and information, press and publicity, and international matters, all run by full-time paid officials. An arrangement that was to last until 1926.

The fall in trade union membership at this time prompted an intensification of the process of consolidation and amalgamation that had begun during the war with the foundation of the British Iron, Steel and Kindred Trades Association in 1917. In 1920 the Union of Post Office Workers was formed and in 1922 fourteen separate unions came together as the Transport & General Workers' Union. Two years later three unions amalgamated to form the General and Municipal Workers' Union.

Trade union matters in the 1920s were to be dominated by the miners. In 1918 the miners emerged from the war demanding a degree of workers' control in an industry they believed should remain nationalised as it had been throughout the war period. In a government fudge to avoid a strike a commission was set up to investigate the matter; it included miners' representatives and several people sympathetic to the miners' cause. The commission's report came down on the side of the miners, recommending that 'the State ownership of the mines be accepted'. But the government chose to ignore the commission's findings and handed the mines back to the coal owners in March 1921. The owners immediately locked out miners who refused to work for lower pay. Fearing disturbances and sympathetic strikes, particularly by the railway and transport workers, the government brought in the troops. In the event no unions came to the miners' aid and they were left to fight on alone.

In 1925 the already battered coal communities received another blow when the coal owners decided to abolish the miners' national minimum wage, cut wages by 10 per cent and maintain profits no matter how low wages fell. As expected the miners refused to accept the changes and the TUC committed itself to sympathetic strike action. To gain time and because it feared serious industrial unrest and a fuel crisis, the government set up another commission to investigate the industry and also agreed to subsidise coal prices for nine months. Some unions scented victory but others were less sure and when the nine months ran out the sceptics were proved right: the coal owners followed the commission's recommendations and reduced wages from 1 May 1926. Two days later the TUC declared that a 'national strike' should begin at one minute to midnight on the 3 May. Over the next nine days about 2 million workers came out in support of the miners. Many local trades councils organised themselves into 'Councils of Action' but nationally there was much confusion among trade unionists made worse by a lack of direction on the part of the TUC General Council who finally called off the strike on 12 May. The miners stayed out till November when, denied any relief, they were starved back to work. In 1927 the government passed a Trades Dispute Act, making general strikes illegal and ensuring union affiliation to the Labour Party became a matter of 'opting in'. This act remained in force until the mines were nationalised in 1946.

In the years that followed the General Strike neither unions nor employers sought confrontation and they even briefly came together in blaming the bankers for the bad state of the economy. However, as the economy continued to deteriorate between 1929 and 1933 industrial strife returned to new levels and the relationship began to falter but not before important lessons had been learnt by both sides. Certainly by the mid-1930s as the economy began to revive both the unions and the employers realised that some degree of cooperation was in their own best interests. Trade unionists who opposed this collaboration – the Communists, for example – often found themselves drummed out of their unions as the whole movement including the Labour Party took a turn to the right.

Hitler's ascent to power in early 1933 sent a cold shiver through Europe's trade union movement. In Britain the TUC quickly drafted a report on 'Dictatorship and the Trade Union Movement' which blamed the Nazis' rise to power on the Communists: it said communist attacks on the unions and the social democrats had fatally weakened the German labour movement. This report was soon followed by a joint Labour Party/TUC manifesto, which declared its opposition to both fascism and communism and recommended that trade unions exclude all communists and fascists from union office. However, in spite of its professed support for German labour, the TUC, along with many local authorities, did embark on a campaign to boycott German goods and in some London schools children were briefly without pencils before another non-German source could be found.

There were other international concerns too. In 1936 fascism was on the march in Spain and many trade unionists rallied to the cause of defending the elected left-wing Popular Front government after General Franco's July coup. While the British government and the TUC supported a policy of non-intervention in the civil war that followed, many unions organised food and medical aid for the republican side. Hundreds of communists and other left-wing trade unionists went to Spain to join the International Brigade to fight alongside the Republican army. After three years the Republicans were finally defeated by a Nationalist army which had been well supported by fascist forces from Italy and Germany throughout the war.

On 3 September 1939 Britain declared war on Germany. At first the government saw no reason to involve the TUC in its war planning but this was to change quickly when, soon after becoming Prime Minister in May 1940, Winston Churchill appointed the General Secretary of the TGWU, Ernest Bevin, as Minister of Labour and National Service. Bevin immediately set up a joint consultative committee of unions and employers and asked unions for their support for the duration of the war; they willingly gave it. He also instituted orders that effectively outlawed strikes by making arbitration in industrial disputes compulsory. This caused the level of strikes to fall to their lowest point since records began. In the interests of war production the trade unions agreed to their members being directed into 'essential undertakings' and to the dropping of restrictive practices. Wage levels rose, there was full employment and trade union membership increased from a pre-war level of about 6 million to nearly 8 million in 1945.

In the general election of April 1945 the Labour Party routed the Tories and the new Prime Minister, Clement Attlee, brought six trade union sponsored MPs (out of 120) into his cabinet: Aneurin Bevan of the miners became Minister of Health, Ernest Bevin of the TGWU became Foreign Secretary, Ellen Wilkinson of the Distribution Workers became Minister of Education, and the Chairman of the TUC, George Isaacs, became Minister of Labour. And as the government embarked on the process of social reconstruction and nationalisation, more and more trade union leaders were appointed to the boards of newly nationalised industries. This integration soon began to create problems for the government and the unions alike on issues such as the restraint of wages and the continuing ban on strikes. Rank-and-file militancy increased as did the number of unofficial strikes, which were blamed on the Communists.

Since the 1920s the Labour Party had seen the presence of Communists in the labour movement as a threat to industrial peace and no more so than when it was in government in the late 1940s. Wherever there was an unofficial strike, for example in the docks disputes of 1947, 1949 and 1950, the Communists were accused at being behind the stoppage. The TUC said the Communists were sabotaging the postwar recovery and in 1949 the TGWU removed all Communists from union office. Although there was little evidence that Communists were the threat that many unions, the TUC and the Labour government imagined, Cold War rhetoric had begun to invade and distort British politics; it was to remain firmly lodged there for the next forty years.

67. 1933. Trades Union Congress.

The Posters 1920–1950

The posters in this section show all too clearly how the twin crises of capitalism – unemployment and fascism – came to dominate many trade union struggles in this period

(68) Since the 1890s there had been several attempts to create a federation of transport unions but this was not achieved until 1920 when, after a ballot of all their members, fourteen separate unions came together on 1 January 1922 to form the Transport & General Workers' Union. Harry Gosling was general secretary of the Amalgamated Society of Watermen, Lightermen and Bargemen and became founding president of the TGWU. He listed 'propaganda' among his interests.

(69) In July 1924 the building employers locked out members of the Amalgamated Union of Building Trade Workers in a dispute over working hours and hourly rates – the union demanded 1d an hour rise the employers offered a ½d. The employers also demanded that the union stamp out indiscipline over working rules.

(70) The National Tailors' Union of Sub-Divisional Workers was a small and short-lived union in London's East End. Emma Goldman was the Lithuanian-born anarchist who the Americans had deported to Russia in 1919 from where she left disillusioned in 1921 and came to England.

(71) It was at this 1927 Rhondda demonstration that the man who had led the miners' through the 1926 General Strike, A.J. Cook, made the call for the first hunger march to draw attention to the dreadful plight of the South Wales miners and their families in the period after the strike was over.

(72) The 'Tory Attack' was the 1927 Trades Dispute Act in which the government banned general strikes and tried to sever the financial links between the trade union movement and the Labour Party in the wake of the General Strike.

(73) Five years after being temporarily expelled from the TUC in 1928 for supporting the right-wing miners' breakaway union during the General Strike, the National Union of Seamen was under new leadership and recruiting as merchant shipping began to recover from the Depression.

(67, 74–87) 1932 and 1933 were busy years for the TUC's propaganda department as it campaigned around the two issues of unemployment and the coming to power of the Nazis in Germany. In 1932 it produced thousands of slogan posters on unemployment and in February 1933, jointly with the National Council of Labour, it distributed posters on the evils of Hitler. In addition it organised a mass meeting against Hitlerism in April at the Albert Hall: 7,000 programmes were sold.

(88–91) In 1934 the TUC celebrated the centenary of the Tolpuddle Martyrs' trial with a grand gala in the Dorset village and using a similar poster launched a campaign to bring more white-collar workers into the union fold. A *Pictorial Souvenir of Tolpuddle* sold 13,000 copies while orders for the 'Cricket' (90) poster produced a year later reached 6,200. The TUC not only shared Transport House with the TGWU but often also shared the same posters.

(92) Tom Mann, the veteran socialist and trade union leader, had been in the forefront of the struggles of the unemployed throughout the 1920s and '30s. Here he is seen in 1936 addressing a meeting of the Arvon Union of the Unemployed in North Wales.

(93–5) Despite significant shortages of paper during the Second World War the TUC managed to produce high quality recruitment posters and other materials, although some valuable poster blocks were lost in a bombing raid in 1940.

(96) Throughout the interwar period and during the Second World War itself much of the trade union movement had wanted the utilities nationalised but it was not until Labour came to power in 1945 that this began to happen. Electricity was nationalised in 1947.

(97–101) The National Union of Distributive and Allied Workers Union (NUDAW) and its forerunners concentrated on organising workers in Co-operative employment. In 1947 it amalgamated with the shop assistants', clerks' and butchers' unions creating the Union of Shop, Distributive and Allied Workers (USDAW).

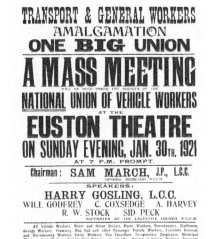

68. 1921. Transport & General Workers' Union.

Amalgamated Union of Building Trade Workers.

NATIONAL DISPUTE

IN THE

BUILDING TRADE, 1924.

To those Members permitted to work during the Dispute.

NO CA' CANNY! IT'S YOUR MONEY WE WANT RIGHT NOW!

Are you doing your bit in the struggle?

Are you paying your levy of 5s. a week to assist the men who are fighting **YOUR** battle as well as their own?

Do you realise that the men in dispute are actually paying a levy of 10s. a week by reduction of Strike Benefit from 30s. to 20s.?

How do you expect to retain your present wages and conditions if the boys are driven back to work by mere starvation?

The man who grumbles and is shirking his responsibilities at this time of crisis is not a friend to his fellow workers, but an enemy. He is playing into the hands of the "bosses."

Whose is the greater hardship? You who, enjoying the fruits of organisation, are earning wages and only called on to sacrifice 5s. a week towards the Strike Fund; or the man on the streets endeavouring to eke out an existence for his family and himself on 20s. a week Strike Benefit?

PLAY THE GAME, BROTHERS!

Don't let your conscience haunt you when the kiddies ask:

"WHAT DID YOU DO IN THE GREAT STRIKE?"

GEORGE HICKS, General Secretary.

Printed by the TWENTIETH CENTURY PRESS 1912, Ltd., T.U. in all Departments, 103, Southwark Street, London, S.E.1. 8751

69. 1924. Amalgamated Union of Building Trade Workers.

70. 1925. National Tailors' Union of Sub-Divisional Workers.

RHONDDA MINERS' DISTRICT & COUNCIL OF ACTION

RED SUNDAY IN RHONDDA VALLEY

Campaign Against BALDWIN & COALOWNERS

MONSTRE RHONDDA

DEMONSTRATION

ON PENRHYS MOUNTAIN

On SUNDAY, SEPTEMBER 18th, at 3 o'clock.

The following Speakers will positively attend :

A. J. COOK

General Secretary, M.F.G.B.

WALL HANNINGTON

National Unemployed, London.

David Lewis, Arthur Horner, W. H. Mainwaring

Miners' District Secretary.　　　　E.C., M.F.G.B.　　　　Miners' Agent.

Chairman: T. THOMAS, Treherbert.

WORKERS, AROUSE! Line Up! Join in the Revolt Against the Coalowners' Government. NOW we want the 1914 Spirit in the Workers' Fight. Organise Your Grumbles and Fight Your Oppressors.

READ THIS TIME TABLE (Men and Women) and Join Your Contingent in this Great March, by falling in behind your Band and Banners.

RHONDDA FACH. Depart from Mardy 1.30 p.m., Ferndale Workmen's Hall 2 p.m., Queen's Square, Tylorstown, 2.30 p.m., Porth Square, Porth, 1.30, Workmen's Hall, Ynyshir, 2 p.m.

RHONDDA FAWR. Depart from Blaenrhondda Station 1 p.m., Bute Square, Treherbert, 1.15 p.m., Stag Square, Treorky, 1.45 p.m., Ystrad Station 2.15, Butchers Arms, Penygraig, 1.30 p.m., Pandy Square, Tonypandy, 2 p.m., Partridge Road, Trealaw, 2.15 p.m.

SPECIAL ATTRACTION! The Mid-Rhondda Section YOUNG COMRADES' LEAGUE and Bands will render Working Class Music and Songs, and lead Mass singing.

Down with Baldwin! On for Workers' Government!

Thomas Bros., Printers, Pandy Square, Tonypandy.

71. 1927. Rhondda Miners' District & Council of Action.

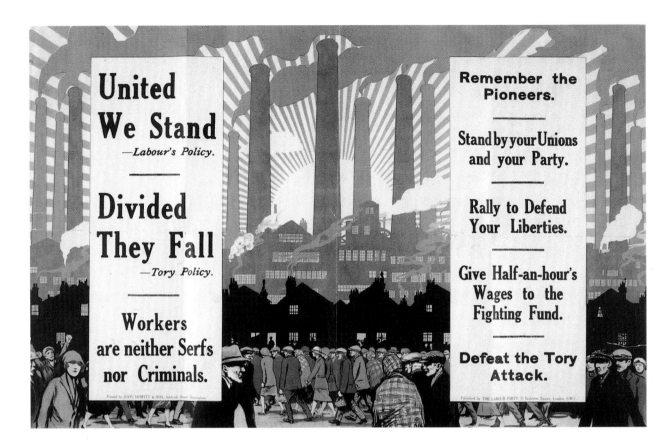

72. 1927. Trades Union Congress.

73. 1934. National Union of Seamen.

MANKIND
SHALL NOT BE
CRUCIFIED
UPON A
CROSS OF
GOLD

WORKLESS MEN
HOARDED MONEY
IDLE MACHINES
SPELL
CAPITALISM

IN TO THE
UNIONS
AND
STAND
TOGETHER

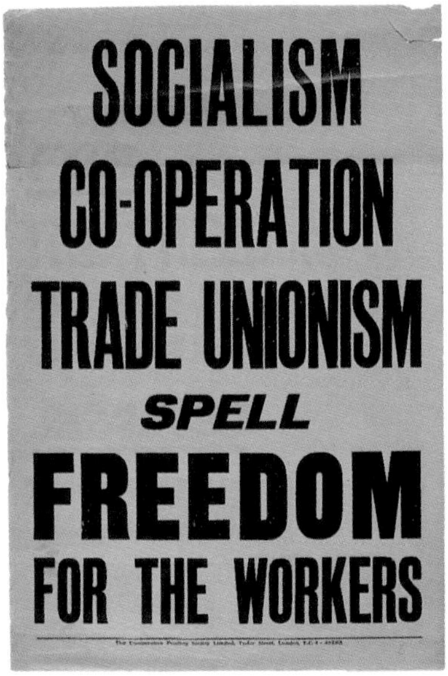

SOCIALISM
CO-OPERATION
TRADE UNIONISM
SPELL
FREEDOM
FOR THE WORKERS

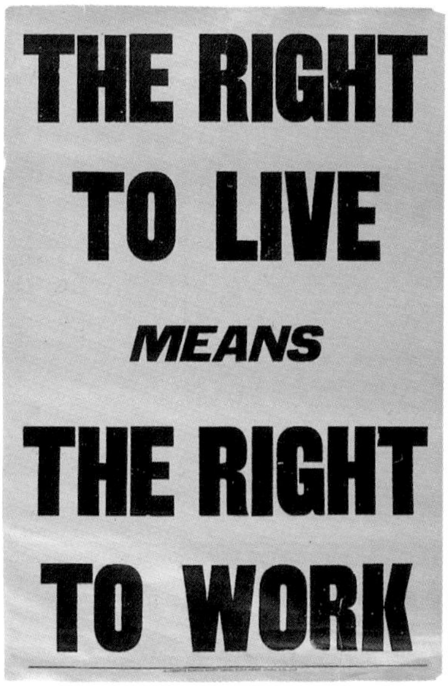

THE RIGHT
TO LIVE
MEANS
THE RIGHT
TO WORK

WORK
OR
MAINTENANCE

IN THE MIDST OF PLENTY WE WILL NOT SUFFER WANT

IDLE ACRES AND WORKLESS MEN THE HUNGRY FORTIES ARE HERE AGAIN

MEN WHO STARVE AT THE FACTORY GATE MARK THE RUIN OF THE STATE

74–82. 1932–3. Trades Union Congress.

83–7. 1933. Trades Union Congress and National Council of Labour call for a boycott of German goods after Hitler comes to power.

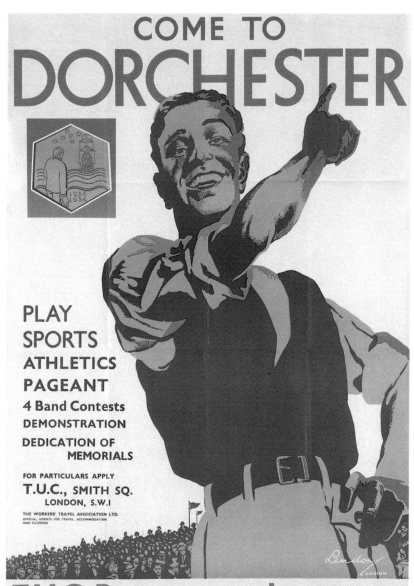

88. 1934. Trades Union Congress.

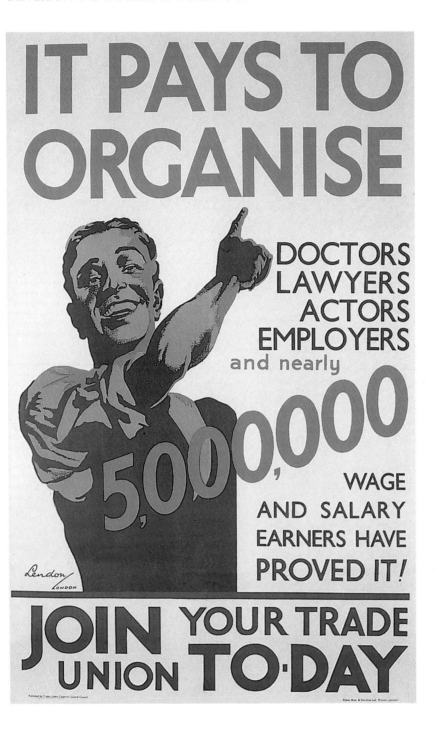

89. 1935. Trades Union Congress.

90. 1934. Trades Union Congress.

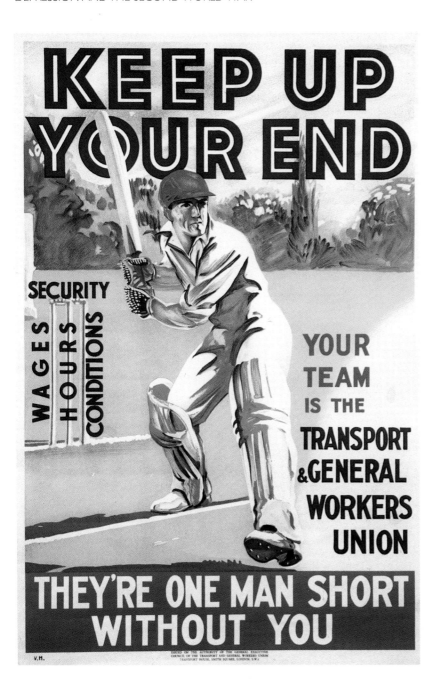

91. 1935. Transport & General Workers' Union.

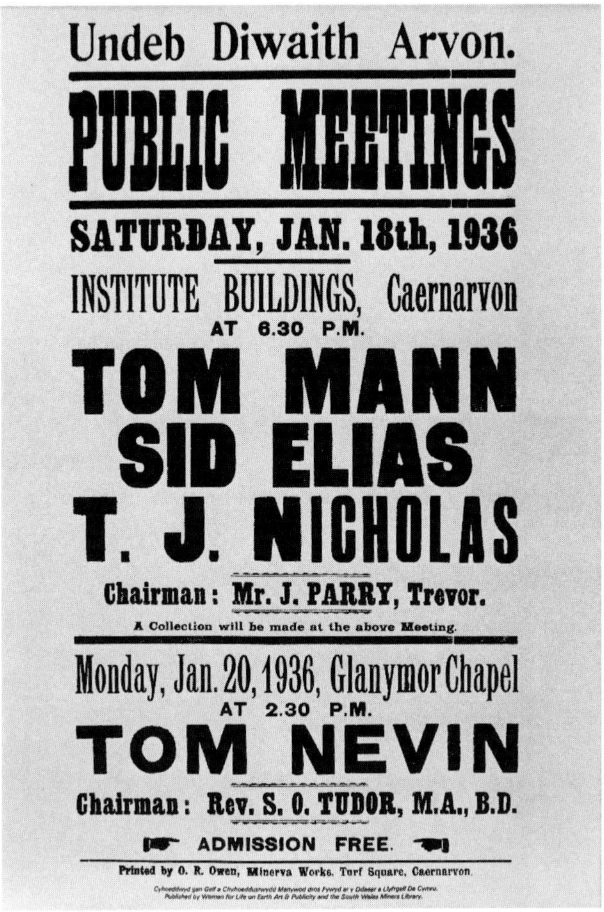

92. 1936. Undeb Diwaith Arvon.

THEN

In 1842 children worked in the mines

NOW

Join your **TRADE UNION**

93. 1942. Trades Union Congress.

94. 1943. Trades Union Congress.

95. 1943. Trades Union Congress.

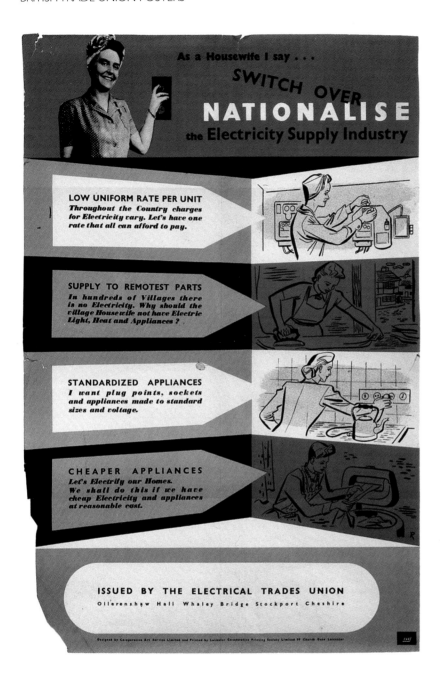

96. 1947. Electrical Trades Union.

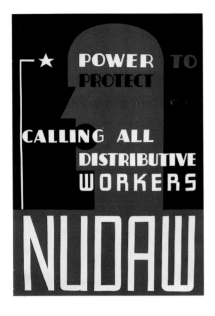

97–100. 1947. National Union of Distributive and Allied Workers.

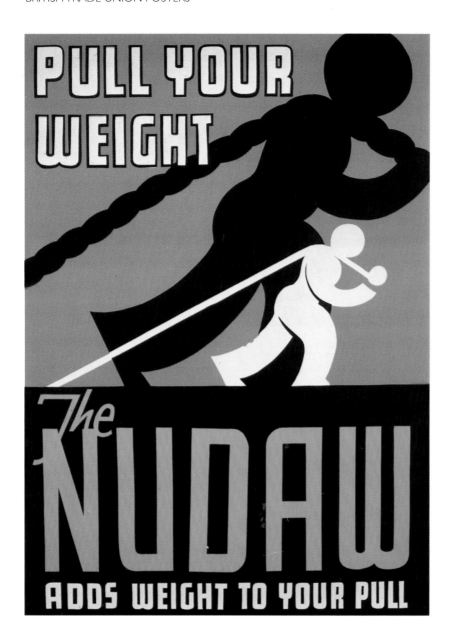

101. 1947. National Union of Distributive and Allied Workers.

Consensus and confrontation

In October 1951 the Labour Party lost the general election to a Conservative Party committed to undoing much of the State's control of the economy built up since 1940. However, this did not mean that wage controls and trade union involvement in government at many levels disappeared. Quite the contrary, in fact, for the new government wished to continue many of the policies that had produced the low levels of industrial dispute under Labour since 1945. But this situation was not to last as low productivity, recurrent balance of payments difficulties and a rise in industrial disputes – particularly in mining, shipbuilding and transport – forced the government and the unions to rethink policy.

By the 1950s the underlying low levels of productivity in British industry brought on by the Second World War and generations of under-investment were becoming clear for all to see. Both sides of industry agreed that something had to done but differed fundamentally on what the right course of action might be. Lessons learnt in the 1940s meant that many unions and the TUC saw increases in productivity as requiring more intervention by the State not less. The employers saw the opposite: increased productivity stemmed from less interference by the State in wage negotiations, speeding up the line and the importation of scientific management techniques from the USA irrespective of the cost to workers. The Conservative government saw the need for selective economic controls but only of wages. Not surprisingly a generation of trade unionists, rightly suspicious of industry's attempts to speed up industrial processes and break down established craft practices, began to fight back and official and unofficial strikes mushroomed.

In 1955 the number of working days lost to strikes rose to twice the 1950 level and the TUC struggled to mediate between employers and workers. A four-week newspaper strike was finally settled only after the TUC and a Court of Inquiry persuaded the newspaper proprietors to make the unions central to the negotiations. Later that year a railway strike was only settled after the TUC acted as a mediator between the two sides. However, the TUC was unable to effect any real movement in the increasing number of unofficial strikes that were taking place, particularly in the docks which had been fraught with problems since the introduction of the Dock Labour Scheme in 1947. Intended to solve the problem of 'casualism' in dock work, the Scheme had pushed up employers' costs which they in turn passed on to the dockers by demanding greater productivity and changes in work practices. Despite a series of successful strikes the dockers' unity against the employers was marred by continuing demarcation disputes and inter-union rivalry. Other unions faced with changes in work practices imposed by employers also had their struggles diluted by inter-union disputes; this was the case with the newspaper printers' and railway workers' strikes in 1955.

Over the next ten years it was the turn of the fast growing motor industry, not noted for its militancy before the war, to take centre stage in industrial disputes. The industry was fragmented, wages differed between plants and the demand for vehicles was both cyclical and seasonal, leaving workers unsure of what was going to be in their next pay packet. Between 1955 and 1965 the number of days per year lost to strikes in the motor industry escalated from 70,000 to 857,000.

Unable or unwilling to control wages effectively in the private sector the government turned on the less well-organised workers in the public sector and in 1957 overruled the independent Whitley Council's pay award to the health workers. Civil servants and those working at the BBC were also subject to government interference in wage negotiations. By contrast in 1958 when faced with demands from the powerful unions in mining, railways and the London buses the government conceded to union demands, making it clear that in industrial disputes, union size and good organisation mattered. This was a situation that was to be reinforced in 1961 when, at the end of a government-imposed, nine-month 'pay pause', the large unions again succeeded in

1950
1980

gaining pay increases while the health workers once more lost out. One result of this growing strength was the government's invitation to some unions and the TUC to join it and employers' representatives in the work of the newly created National Economic Development Council whose job it was to help government achieve national economic targets.

In the late 1950s the increased presence of large trade unions also affected the whole movement's relations with Labour Party and the conduct of its Annual Conference. Almost since the trade union movement gave birth to the Labour Party in the 1890s the unions had been able to influence party policy at Conference through the block-vote system. The block-vote system had often been challenged by both right and left in the party and had led to frequent accusations, particularly by the right-wing press and the Conservative Party, that the Labour Party was 'undemocratic'.

When the Labour Party led by Harold Wilson was returned to power in 1964, the trade union movement with its 10.25 million members was determined to be a force in the new government's economic planning. Its hopes were realised when, within months, the unions signed a joint statement on incomes, prices and productivity with the government and the employers. But it was not long before this new relationship came under severe strain: in 1966, in the face of serious opposition from the unions and the TUC, the government imposed a wage freeze followed by a period of 'severe restraint'. The situation continued to deteriorate, reaching an all-time low when the government published *In Place of Strife*, its White Paper on industrial relations, in 1969. To the TUC and the unions the White Paper confirmed that the Labour government, like the Conservatives before it, was seeking to lay the sole blame for Britain's industrial decline on union restrictive practices, collective bargaining and widespread unofficial strikes. This anti-union attitude, combined with a failure to achieve significant growth in the economy, contributed to Labour's defeat in the June 1970 general election.

The new Conservative government under Edward Heath wasted no time in trying to correct the chaos in industrial relations it believed it had inherited from Labour and quickly sought to bring on to the statute book a new Industrial Relations Act. The Act set up the National Industrial Relations Court (NIRC) with wide-ranging powers, able to impose pre-strike ballots, 'cooling-off' periods and substantial fines for 'unfair industrial practices'. It also required unions to register with the new Registrar of Trade Unions and Employers' Associations and banned the pre-entry closed shop. All these measures were based on the government's belief (shared with the previous Labour administration) that the unions had let shop stewards gain control of their members which in turn had led to the many unofficial strikes that were crippling the economy.

The unions and the TUC strongly objected to the new Act seeing it as a major challenge to the voluntary system that had, with all its weaknesses, prevailed since 1945. Rallies and demonstrations were held around the country and the TUC organised a major demonstration in London under the banner of 'Attack Injustice'. Following a Special Congress the TUC advised unions to boycott the NIRC and not to register. However, thirty-two unions did register and this resulted in their being suspended at the 1972 TUC Congress: during the following year twenty of these were eventually expelled.

1972 was a bad year for the Tory government. Its much-vaunted new industrial relations laws showed themselves to be rather toothless when tested in court. Its statutory pay policy was also to come under considerable strain when confronted by a miners' strike in January and February, a strike which resulted in a state of emergency and a three-day week being declared. Ultimately the miners were victorious. This defeat for the government was coupled with the humiliation that followed the brief imprisonment in July of the 'Pentonville Five' – a move which brought 170,000 dockers

102. 1954. Civil servants outside the Houses of Parliament demonstrating for equal pay for women.

out on strike in July and prompted the intervention of the little-known Official Solicitor to gain their release. The government's industrial relations policy was falling into tatters. Eighteen months later it was confronted with another strike by the miners and was forced to call a general election in February 1974 under the slogan 'Firm Action for a Fair Britain'. The Conservatives lost to a minority Labour government led by Harold Wilson.

In opposition the Labour Party had promised to repeal the hated Industrial Relations Act and bring about a new voluntary partnership with the unions – the 'Social Contract'. In return a Labour government would take action to limit prices and rents and to transform the tax system by 'squeezing the rich till the pips squeaked'. Once in government the Labour administration settled the miners' claim and introduced the Trade Union and Labour Relations Bill to replace the Industrial Relations Act. In September 1974 the TUC Congress voted in favour of the 'Social Contract' thereby agreeing to seek pay rises in line with the rise in the cost of living after tax.

Inflation eased in the summer and early autumn leading Wilson to call another general election in October in the belief that he could win with a larger majority. But this was not to be. Although the Labour Party increased its number of seats its overall majority was only three. The Conservative Party was in disarray and in February 1975 replaced Edward Heath with Margaret Thatcher as leader.

The next two years saw the Labour government struggle to contain inflation and steep rises in unemployment by austerity budgets and the transfer of public resources into the private sector. In the summer of 1975 wage increases were limited to £6. But things went from bad to worse: in December the government faced a sterling crisis and was forced to approach the International Monetary Fund (IMF) to secure a massive a loan. A year later the government cut public expenditure further in return for another and even greater loan from the IMF. Unemployment continued to rise and industrial relations worsened although stoppages at work remained at a low level.

Since Labour came to power in 1974 much of the press had been hostile to trade union involvement in the corridors of power, dubbing the relationship as one of 'beer and sandwiches at Number 10' and accusing the government of allowing the 'big' unions to call the tune. When the 'Social Contract' finally became unworkable in 1977, the unions were blamed and some commentators even saw them as a threat to parliamentary democracy itself. Scenes of disorderly picketing at the Grunwick photo-processing plant in north London, particularly with the presence of the Yorkshire miners in support, gave the right wing a field day. A nine-week strike at Ford in August 1978 was followed later in the year by strikes involving local authority workers, railway workers and others: all were fodder for a media campaign against the unions headlined the 'Winter of Discontent'. The Labour government did little or nothing to counter the demonising of the unions by the Tories and it was no surprise that at the general election in May 1979 the Tories under Margaret Thatcher swept to power on an anti-union ticket.

103. 1978. National Association of Local Government Officers.

The Posters 1950–1980

In the thirty years after the end of the Second World War trade unions moved from being a part of government to being seen as the cause of national economic decline. Unions and both Labour and Tory governments fought over anti-union legislation and the decline of traditional industries as some of the posters in this section show.

(103) One of the benefits of belonging to a large union in the time before cheap overseas holidays was that many of the larger organisations had holiday accommodation of their own at English seaside resorts like the one advertised here for NALGO members at Croyde Bay in North Devon.

(104–18) As rationing ended and shops began to stock more goods there was pressure on shopkeepers to stay open longer. One of USDAW's major tasks was to ensure that 1950 Shops Act fully protected the interests of its members. In 1951 USDAW had 347,737 members but found that a quarter of these lapsed every year, most of them to join an employer where the union did not organise. However, to ensure that these lost members were replaced by an equal number or more – which they were – it campaigned constantly with high quality posters encouraging new recruits from workplaces where it already had members.

(119) The Durham Gala has been one of the great celebrations of the trade union movement since it was first held in 1883. Clement Attlee was Prime Minister 1945–51 and Leader of the Opposition 1951–5; he was replaced by Hugh Gaitskill after the defeat of Labour at the May 1955 General Election.

(120–3) Recruitment posters drawn and designed by Ken Sprague and printed by John Gorman's company G&B Arts.

(124) The writings of William Morris, the nineteenth-century socialist and designer, have been an inspiration to the labour and trade union movement since his involvement in revolutionary politics in the1880s.

(125) This TGWU poster arguing for a minimum wage of £15 ran the risk of being banned because it is illegal to reproduce bank notes in any way.

(126–8) Ernest Bevin was general secretary of the TGWU 1921–40, Minister of Labour 1940–5 and Foreign Secretary 1945–51. Frank Cousins was general secretary of the TGWU 1956–66, and between 1964 and 1966 he was seconded to the Labour government as Minister of Technology. The recruitment poster echoes the socialist graphics of 1920s.

(129) In July 1971 the Tory government decided to liquidate the Upper Clyde Shipbuilders (UCS) with the loss of 6,000 jobs. The workers occupied the yards, and widespread support for their cause from the labour and trade union movement and from the public led to a victory by the unions.

(130–2, 134, 135) Edward Heath's 1970–4 Tory administration's attitude to the unions in general, and its Industrial Relations Act in particular, brought understanding between government and the trade union movement to a new low. In February 1971 the TUC organised a mass demonstration against the bill under the banner of 'Attack Injustice'. In January 1972 the miners came out on strike for six weeks and this resulted in the government declaring a state of emergency and a three-day week. In July five dockers were arrested and briefly imprisoned for picketing bringing thousands of dockers on to the streets in protest. Inspired by the UCS occupation, the print workers of Briant Colour Printing in south London organised an eleven-month work-in after being given one minute's notice when the company went into liquidation.

(136) After 1978, the TGWU women's delegate conference became an annual event and women in the union, whatever their age, were addressed as women.

(137) Tory governments have never been in favour of public transport and in the 1970s the TGWU campaigned against the cut in subsidies to buses that led to higher fares and a reduction in services.

(138, 139) As the music business mushroomed in the 1970s the Musicians' Union stepped up its recruitment campaign in order to protect musicians' employment opportunities against the threat from the increased use of tapes and records. The campaign gave rise to the union's slogan 'Keep Music Live'.

(140) On the fiftieth anniversary of the 1926 General Strike the TUC mounted a major exhibition in London to commemorate the event.

(141–4) As the retail sector boomed in the late 1970s so USDAW stepped up its recruitment campaigns, using images from sports which were themselves beginning to boom in popularity. However, it is interesting to note that the sports chosen are largely male-dominated despite the fact that at the time the majority of USDAW members were women.

(145) By putting a child at the centre of this poster the designer Ken Sprague is emphasising that the National Union of Teachers' fair pay campaign put the interests of the children first.

(147, 148) The long industrial dispute at the Grunwick photo-processing factory in north London lasted from August 1976 to July 1978 and was among the most important of the decade. The company employed mostly Asian women at a third of the average industrial wage and overtime was compulsory. The sacking of a worker and a row over overtime prompted a strike by 137 workers led by Jayaben Desai. In the ensuing struggle pickets at the factory were joined by thousands of fellow trade unionists, Labour ministers and MPs but the management, supported by right-wing organisations like the National Association for Freedom, held firm and bussed in blacklegs every day. The strike was finally abandoned and the company continued to employ non-union workers at low wages.

(149, 150) Throughout the 1970s the National Union of Agricultural Workers used Ken Sprague's strong images in its long-running campaign to persuade workers that tied cottages were being used by many employers to keep down their wages. Tied cottages also represented a real threat to workers and their families in a time when the number of agricultural jobs was continuing to fall. 'Evictions break hearts as well as homes' – out of a job could also mean being homeless.

(151) Local government expenditure and jobs were in the front line of cuts imposed by Margaret Thatcher's government within months of coming to power in May 1979.

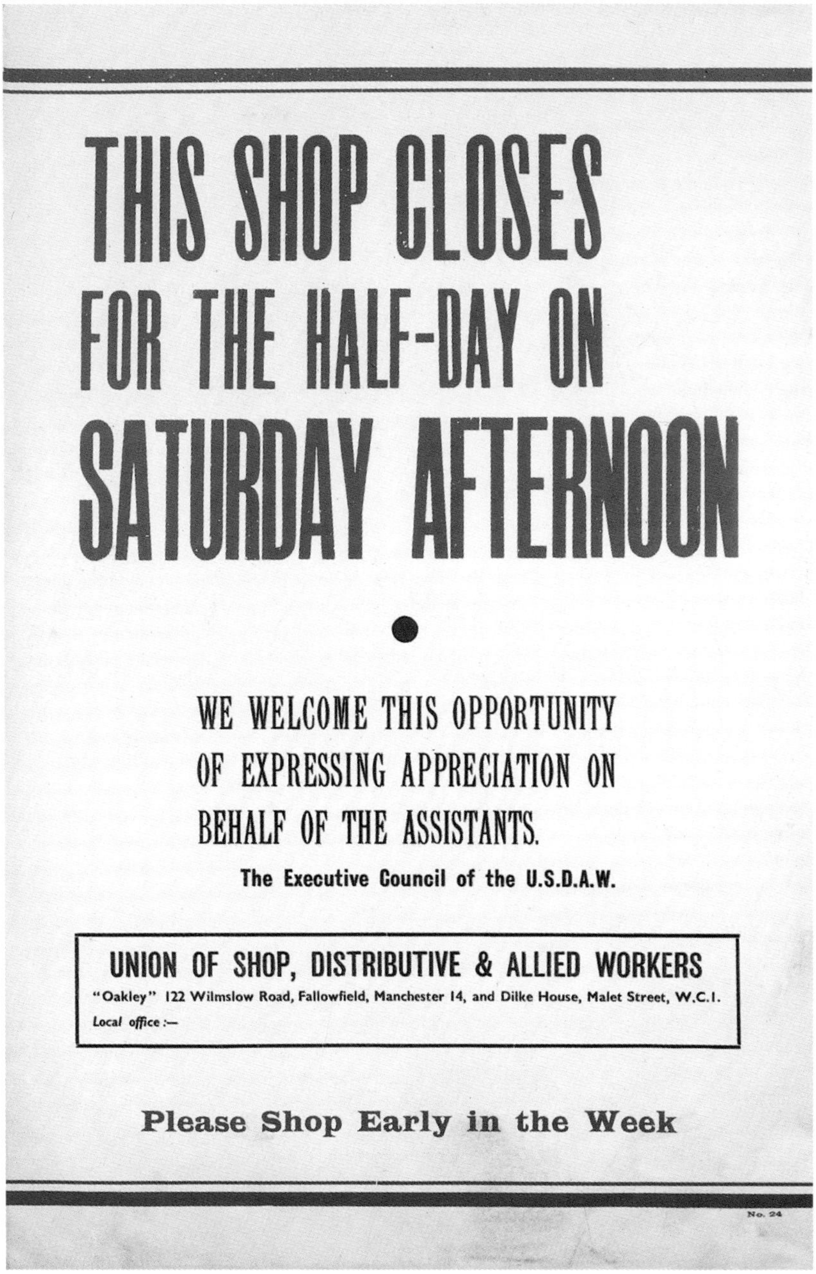

THIS SHOP CLOSES
FOR THE HALF-DAY ON
SATURDAY AFTERNOON

●

WE WELCOME THIS OPPORTUNITY
OF EXPRESSING APPRECIATION ON
BEHALF OF THE ASSISTANTS.

The Executive Council of the U.S.D.A.W.

UNION OF SHOP, DISTRIBUTIVE & ALLIED WORKERS
"Oakley" 122 Wilmslow Road, Fallowfield, Manchester 14, and Dilke House, Malet Street, W.C.1.
Local office :—

Please Shop Early in the Week

No. 24

104. 1950. Union of Shop, Distributive and Allied Workers.

105. 1950. Union of Shop, Distributive and Allied Workers.

106. 1950. Union of Shop, Distributive and Allied Workers.

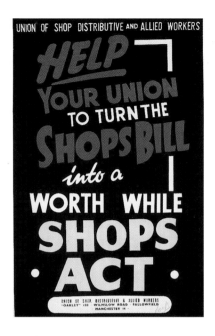

107–10. 1950. Union of Shop, Distributive and Allied Workers.

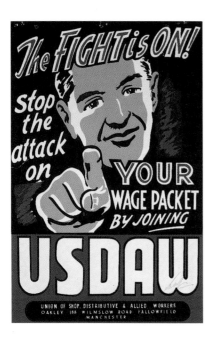

111–14. 1951. Union of Shop, Distributive and Allied Workers.

115. 1952. Union of Shop, Distributive and Allied Workers.

116. 1952. Union of Shop, Distributive and Allied Workers.

117. 1953. Union of Shop, Distributive and Allied Workers.

118. 1955. Union of Shop, Distributive and Allied Workers.

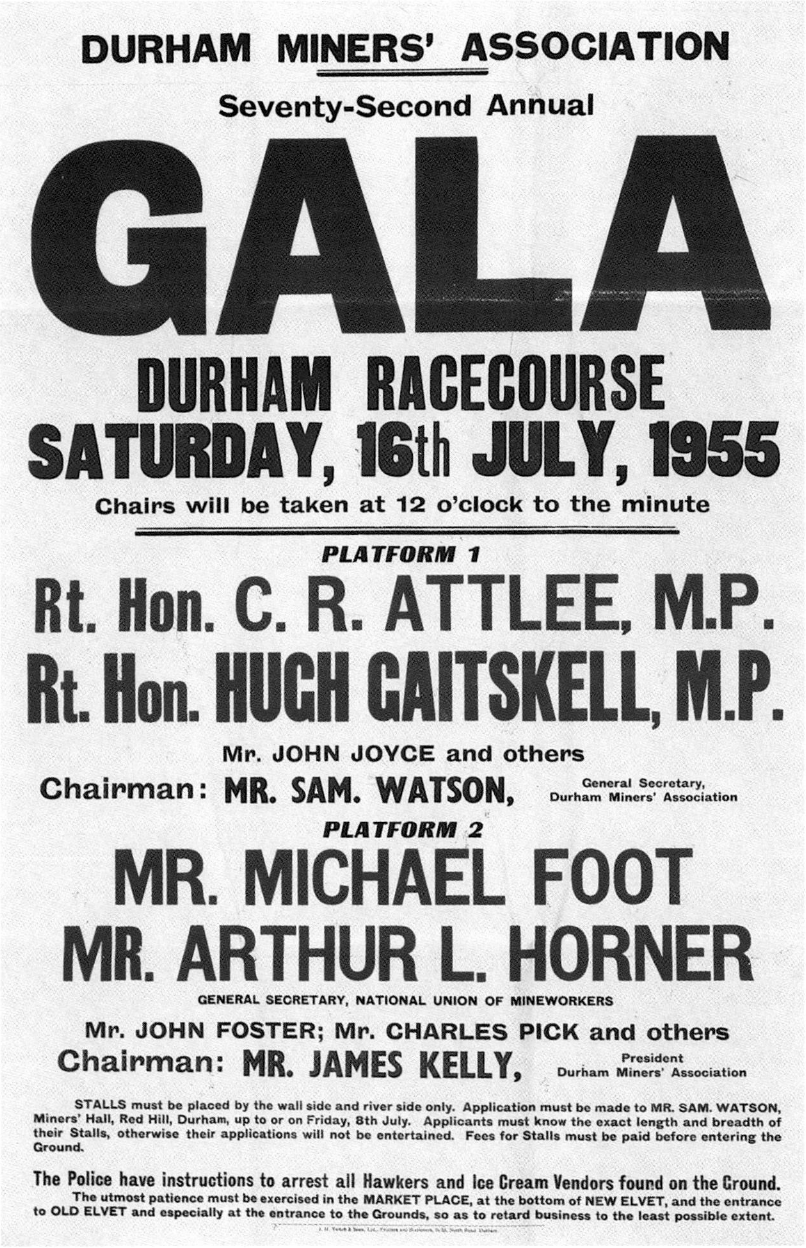

119. 1955. Durham Miners' Association.

120. n.d. Amalgamated Union of Engineering Workers.
121. n.d. National Union of Tailors and Garment Workers.
122. n.d. National Union of Agricultural Workers.
123. n.d. National Union of Tailors and Garment Workers.

124. 1965. Amalgamated Engineering Union.

125. n.d. Transport & General Workers' Union.

126. 1966. Transport & General Workers' Union.

127. 1966. Transport & General Workers' Union.

128. 1966. Transport & General Workers' Union.

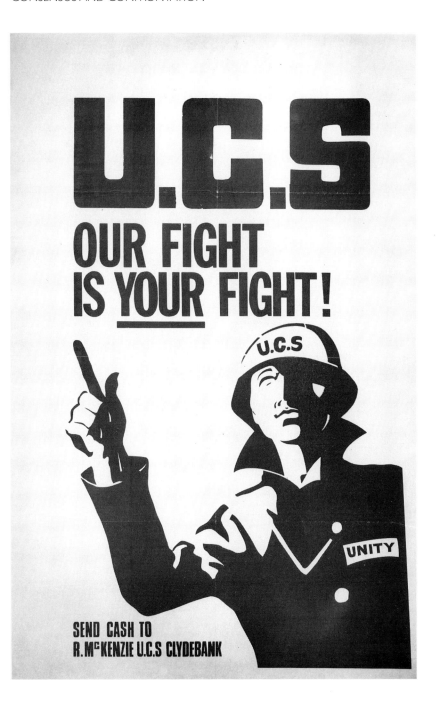

129. 1971. Upper Clyde Shipbuilders, Shop Stewards' Co-ordinating Committee.

130. 1971. Transport & General Workers' Union.

131. 1971. TUC demonstration against the Tories' Industrial Relations Bill.

132. 1972. Briant Colour workers.

Opposite: 133. 1972. Dockers march for the release of the 'Pentonville Five'.

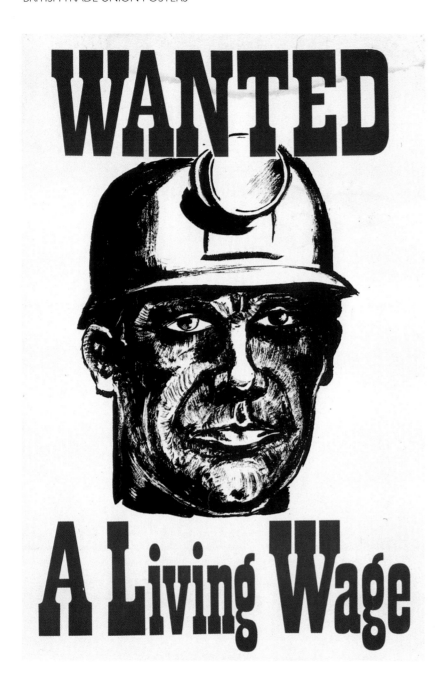

134. 1972. National Union of Mineworkers.

135. 1972. National Union of Mineworkers.

136. 1973. Transport & General Workers' Union.

137. 1973. Transport & General Workers' Union.

138. n.d. Musicians' Union.

139. n.d. Musicians' Union.

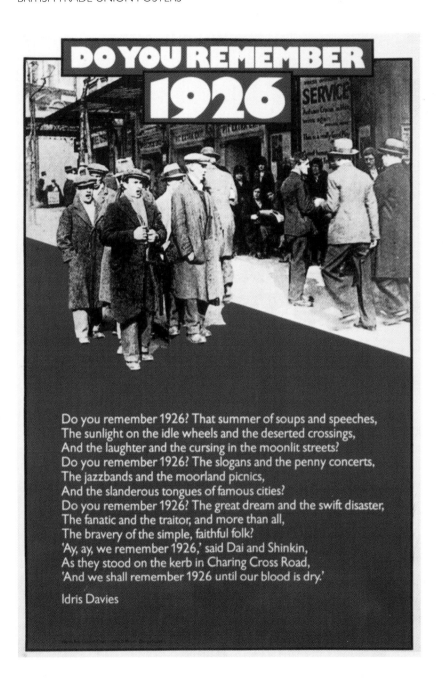

140. 1976. Trades Union Congress.

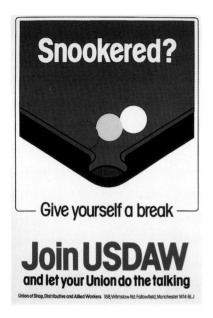

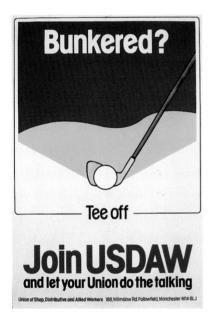

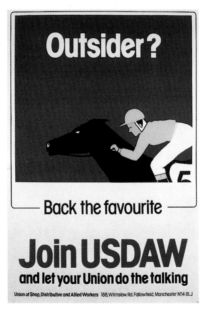

141– 4. 1976. Union of Shop, Distributive and Allied Workers.

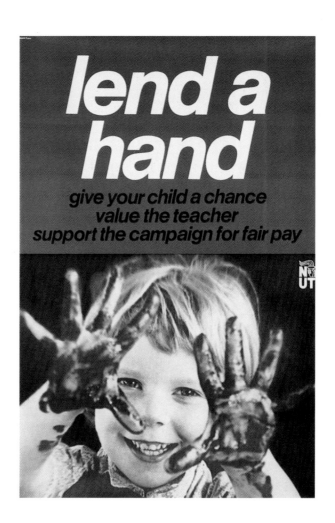

145. n.d. National Union of Teachers.

Opposite: 146. 1976. Grunwick workers picket outside their factory.

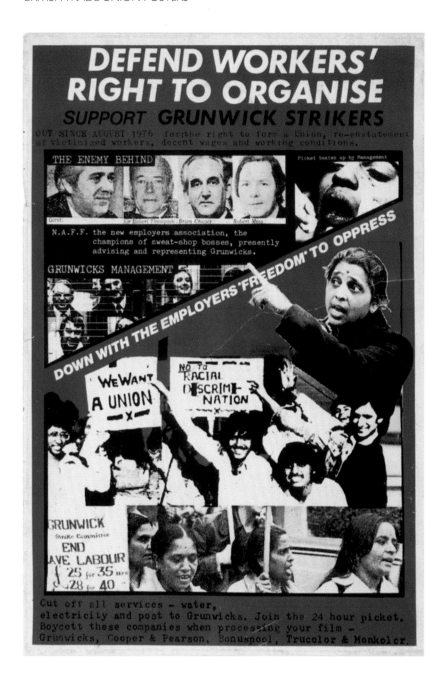

147. 1976. Brent Trades Council.

148. 1978. Dan Jones.

149. 1976. National Agricultural Workers' Union.

150. 1976. National Agricultural Workers' Union.

151. 1979. National Association of Local Government Officers.

Thatcherism and New Labour

After the humiliation of the Heath government at the hands of the miners in 1972 many Tories both inside and outside Parliament spoke of the need to 'reform and modernise' the trade unions. It was, therefore, no surprise that when they came to power in May 1979 under Margaret Thatcher the Conservatives set about the reforms with some vigour. Informed by a free-market philosophy that stressed the rights of the individual over the collective, the new government's first move was to issue a consultative document that called for a ban on secondary picketing, increased exemptions from the closed shop, secret ballots before strikes and the election of full-time trade union officials. Initial discussions between the government and the TUC broke down in March 1980 after the TUC called for a 'Day of Action' on 14 May to protest against the government's policies. In the summer the new policies were made law in the 1980 Employment Act.

Besides wishing to weaken the unions the government also adopted, after setting up various wage reviews, a strict pay policy in the nationalised industries and when it attempted to impose a pay settlement on workers in the steel industry in 1980 the workers came out on strike. After a three-month struggle, the steelworkers gained a substantial increase only to see their industry slowly strangled by falling orders as work went to overseas suppliers. Attempts were made to resurrect a new 'Triple Alliance' of the transport workers, miners and railway workers to defend the steelworkers but, in the event, closures and large-scale redundancies quickly followed.

In the autumn of 1981 the moderate James Prior was replaced by the acerbic Norman Tebbit as Secretary of State for Employment. Tebbit swiftly showed his anti-union credentials in the 1982 Employment Act which banned the pre-entry closed shop and required a closed shop to be supported by 85 per cent of those voting. Tebbit also issued a Green Paper suggesting compulsory secret ballots for the election of union general secretaries and before strikes could be authorised. But most important of all the Green Paper sought to break the ties between the unions and the Labour Party by requiring union members to contract-in – as opposed to contract-out – when paying their political levy to the party. In 1986 when the unions were forced to vote on the issue they gave their overwhelming support for retaining the *status quo* thereby maintaining the financial links upon which Labour Party funds were so dependent.

In the first three years of the Thatcher government unemployment rose from 1 million to over 3 million as the policies of creating 'a leaner and fitter Britain' cut swathes through public and private industries alike. As a consequence trade union membership fell from its all-time high of 13.3 million in 1979 to 11.6 million in 1982 and showed every sign of falling further. Although thoroughly committed to fighting the government's de-industrialisation policies and privatisation of the public utilities, the TUC and many unions were hesitant about what to do with the unemployed. Attempts by the Labour-controlled Greater London Council to fund a local trade union resource centre were disallowed by the TUC which feared that it would drive a wedge between unions and their members. Efforts to set up a special unemployment section within the TUC also failed to attract support from affiliated unions.

As though on cue the Tories endeavoured to turn the country's attention away from the industrial crisis and mass unemployment that its unremitting free-market policies were bringing about by banging the patriotic drum; in April 1982 Britain went to war with Argentina over the Falkland Islands. The war lasted just over two months and cost more than 1,000 British and Argentinian lives. A year after the British victory the government held a general election at which the number of Labour seats in the House of Commons were reduced to 209 from the 269 it held after1979. In 1984 the Tory Government banged the patriotic drum once again when it banned workers at the Government Communications Headquarters at Cheltenham from being members of a union on the grounds that union membership was incompatible with 'national security'.

Although government policies on industrial relations were dramatically driving down the number of working days lost to industrial disputes, some spectacular confrontations with the unions were in the offing. The first of these was in 1983 when the National Graphical Association (NGA) tried to impose a closed shop at Eddie Shah's print works in Warrington. Shah resisted the union's picketing by taking out a court injunction. When the action continued the courts fined the union for contempt and sequestered its assets. In spite of a national newspaper strike on the 24 December 1983 the NGA was forced to admit defeat in order to regain control of its assets.

But the most important industrial conflict of this period was to be between the government, the National Coal Board and the mineworkers. The stage was set for a confrontation when the millionaire American industrialist Ian MacGregor, fresh from a three-year stint destroying the steel industry, was appointed as the new chairman of the Coal Board in September 1983. Almost immediately MacGregor offered the miners a 5.2 per cent wage increase – which they rejected – and imposed an overtime ban. On the 5 March MacGregor told the miners that he intended to cut coal output with a loss of some 20,000 jobs. Four days later the miners' struck in Yorkshire, Scotland and Kent and sent flying pickets to other areas to persuade working miners to join in. Mass picketing led to confrontations with the police, most notably at the Ollerton pit where one miner was killed in the crush and at the Orgreave coke plant. As the strike continued throughout 1984 public support for the miners grew although official support among other unions was very variable. A split among the miners opened up when a substantial number of those who worked the Nottinghamshire fields set up the rival Union of Democratic Mineworkers which sought to negotiate with the government.

The winter of 1984/5 passed without power cuts and the strike began to crumble when 15,000 miners returned to work after being offered a Christmas bonus. However, the position of those miners who stayed out and their families remained acute, bringing many women in mining communities into political action for the first time. Eventually the strikers had to admit defeat and at the end of February 1985 the Welsh miners returned to work. A month later a special delegate meeting of miners agreed to a return to work after fifty-one weeks on strike. Little had been gained by the longest strike in British mining history for the government continued to close pits and sell off the rump of the industry. By 1997 the membership of the National Union of Mineworkers had fallen from 249,711 members in 1982 to a mere 9,565.

Further changes were afoot in the newspaper industry too as new technology forced the print unions into conflict with a new breed of press baron. At no point was this more clear than in January 1986 when Rupert Murdoch's News International Group – owners of *The Times*, the *Sunday Times*, the *Sun*, and the *News of the World* – dismissed 5,500 workers after they refused to sign up to new working arrangements, a no-strike agreement and a move from Fleet Street to a new site at Wapping in London's East End. Over the ensuing months 'Murdoch's fortress' at Wapping was picketed by strikers and fines and threats were regularly meted out to the unions. Finally, after a violent mass picket and demonstration on the anniversary of the strike Murdoch threatened court action to sequester unions funds and the strike collapsed. That Murdoch was able to run his new plant throughout the dispute with the aid of members of the Electrical, Electronic, Telecommunication and Plumbing Union led to the EEPTU being expelled at the TUC Congress in 1988.

The struggle of women for full recognition in a male-dominated trade union movement has been long and drawn out, despite the fact that the TUC has held an annual Women's Conference since 1931. Since the Second World War women workers have provided the largest source of recruitment for trade unions, mainly as a result of the growth of local and national government, the National Health Service and office work but in 1982 women still only comprised 28 per cent of total TUC affiliated membership. At the 1979 TUC Congress only three resolutions out of a total of 113 referred specifically to women. Even after the passing of the Sex Discrimination and Equal Pay Acts in 1975 many unions were slow to treat women's equality issues

152..1980. TUC Day of Action against the Tory government's anti-union Employment Act. NATSOPA's Reg Brady addresses a meeting outside the *Daily Express* building in Fleet Street.

seriously. In the early 1980s it was often said that male trade unionists had grown accustomed to the language of feminism and had learnt how to avoid accusations of 'chauvinism'. However, as Tory policies cut deeper into the male-dominated traditional industries more and more women were coming into the labour market. Increased female membership in unions like NUPE, NALGO and COHSE (Confederation of Health Service Employees and UNISON after 1993) and the teaching unions began pushing women's issues further up the agenda of the whole movement – the TUC established an Equal Rights Department in 1988 – but women still remained a minority in high union office. In 1997 out of seventy-three unions affiliated to the TUC, only five had women general secretaries while the ten unions with a majority of women members still had men holding this position. In the same year only a third of the TUC General Council were women although women made up just over a half of all members of TUC-affiliated unions.

Between 1980 and 1997, when they were finally voted out of office, the Tory government passed nine Acts that directly affected the daily work and conduct of trade unions and their members. To put this in perspective the 1974–9 Labour government had managed only two Acts, its Tory predecessor one, and in the seventy years prior to that there had only been the 1927 Trades Dispute Act and that had been repealed by the postwar Labour government in 1946. This new climate of anti-union legislation inevitably led to some passivity in much of the trade union movement as intransigent employers turned to the courts to resolve industrial relations.

Throughout the almost twenty years of Tory government, first under Margaret Thatcher and then John Major, many trade unionists pinned their hopes of a change on the election of a Labour government. They had to wait for the new regime until May 1997 when New Labour under Tony Blair swept to power with the biggest majority since 1945. Hopes of a change in union status were high but it soon became apparent that New Labour valued its friends in industry and the city more than those in the unions. Unions, the new Government declared, would be treated no differently from any other organisations and there would certainly be no return to the 'beer and sandwiches' days of the Wilson years. As this book went to print New Labour was still maintaining most of the anti-union legislation of the Tories – some in violation of International Labour Organisation conventions to which Britain is a signatory – and had failed to bring the minimum wage up to the modest level demanded by the unions. Meanwhile, hope was on the horizon for the unions and those in work as a raft of legislation from the European Parliament, notably the Social Chapter, began to improve working conditions as did the Government's Fairness at Work measures that at least offered the legal right of union recognition in some workplaces.

However, the trade union movement now faced a major problem of recruitment with its membership down by half since 1980. Particularly challenging for the unions was the problem of recruiting workers under thirty and those in the fastest growing sectors of the economy like new technology. In 1998 strike levels were extremely low but those trade unionists who ventured out, like the postal and rail workers, did well. This success, along with, for example, the resistance of teaching unions to performance-related pay, may well presage a collision between the trade union movement and the Labour government in the new millennium.

The Posters 1980–2000

The posters in this section show how the trade union movement was often the victim of a concerted campaign against its very existence by a succession of Tory governments and employers. However, although the postwar consensus was over and the Welfare State under threat, workers in a whole range of industries continued to make their voices heard.

(153) Influenced by the recent New York health workers two-year cultural project 'Bread and Roses', the TUC mounted its own modest event of the same name in April/May 1980. A small exhibition at Congress House was followed by a rally at the Theatre Royal, Drury Lane, with entertainment by Rik Mayall, Ruby Wax, George Melly, John Wells and Willy Rushton and short speeches by Neil Kinnock, Clive Jenkins, Trevor Phillips and Prunella Scales on how the fight for 'Roses' is as important as the one for 'Bread'.

(154) The trade union movement's first major public confrontation with Margaret Thatcher's anti-union policies came on the 14 May 1980 when the TUC's 'Day of Action' brought thousands on to the streets in a mass protest against the proposed 1980 Employment Bill.

(155, 156) The garment workers protested at the effects of Tory policies – the destruction of jobs in the clothing trade and the erosion of the health service.

(157) In Northern Ireland for decades jobs and whole industries, like shipbuilding, had been divided along sectarian lines and as the brutal civil war between Catholics and Protestants continued into the early 1980s the trade union movement campaigned against the intimidation of workers, knowing it to be a cause of industrial decline and of the lack of much needed new investment.

(158) Since the 1950s many trade unions had adopted policies calling for the abolition of nuclear weapons. The campaign against Britain's continued deployment of nuclear weapons and the presence of American nuclear bases was given an added impetus when Margaret Thatcher agreed to the Americans siting cruise missiles at Greenham Common in the early 1980s.

(159, 162) The image that public services were being 'attacked' or 'killed-off' by Tory policies

was a common theme on many posters and handbills produced in the 1980s. Words like 'Kill', 'Smash' and 'Kick' and the more passive 'Defend' were directed at the government and were also frequently seen as reflecting the anger felt by many at the destruction of much-valued public services.

(160) In May 1981 county council elections Labour swept to power around the country. The Tories put their defeat down to mid-term unpopularity but were soon to see the new councils as a threat to their power and nowhere more so than in the capital where the Greater London Council and the Inner London Education Authority (ILEA) held sway. Kenneth Baker, as Minister of Local Government and later Secretary of State for the Environment, was instrumental in bringing about the abolition of both the GLC and the ILEA in 1986 and dividing up their responsibilities among the London boroughs.

(161) Hotel and catering workers, who are often from ethnic minorities and unaware of their rights, are very badly paid and may not have English as their first language. In the 1970s and '80s the International Branch of the TGWU campaigned for better conditions and the unionisation of these workers.

(163, 164) Margaret Thatcher's policy of 'rolling back the frontiers of the State' led to large sections of local government services being privatised. Along with placing severe restraint on council budgets, these measures made services like waste disposal, direct works and community care subject to compulsory competitive tendering which frequently resulted in workers being made redundant or being offered worse pay and conditions by private contractors. In 1984 British Telecom was among the first of the major public utilities to be sold off.

(165) The National Association of Local Government Officers was among the first unions to adopt a policy that fought for equal rights for lesbian and gay people in the workplace.

(166–174) The 1984/5 miners' strike was one of the bitterest in British postwar history. The government and the Coal Board, led by the American millionaire Ian MacGregor, were bent on defeating the miners after they came

out on strike in March 1984. But the miners stood firm for almost a year before returning to work the following March. The miners' claim that the government was committed to closing down most of the British coal industry was proved right for by the mid-1990s an industry that had employed more than ¼ million workers in 1984 was reduced to less than 3,000 by 1994 and had been privatised.

(175) Racism is endemic in much of British society and by the 1980s it had become vital for the trade union movement to address the issue within its own ranks. In a climate where several Tory ministers espoused near racist views and implemented racist immigration policies many unions, including the National Union of Journalists, campaigned for more racial equality and justice.

(176) Eleanor Marx was the youngest daughter of Karl Marx, a key figure in British socialist and trade union politics in the 1880s, and a mentor to Will Thorne, the young gas workers' leader. Like her father she showed a great interest in Irish politics and was active among Irish groups in Britain. She committed suicide in 1898 aged forty-three.

(178) When Rupert Murdoch's News International Group sacked 5,500 workers in January 1986 for refusing to sign up to new working arrangements the print unions called

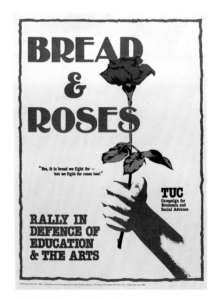

153. 1980. Trades Union Congress

for a boycott of all NIG newspapers. The XXXX is a reference to the then current advertising campaign by Castlemaine, a well-known brand of Australian lager.

(179) Despite countrywide opposition the Tories pushed through their Poll Tax measures in the 1988 Local Government Finance Act. The extensive agitations and refusals to register surrounding the Poll Tax contributed to the downfall of Margaret Thatcher on 29 November 1990.

(184) 1988 May Day Celebration organised by Edinburgh Trades Council.

(185) In 1988, on the fifth anniversary of the Tory government's banning of trade unions from Government Communications Headquarter at Cheltenham, the TUC and Council of Civil Service Unions held a 'GCHQ Day' to remind fellow trade unionists that the sacked workers were still fighting for reinstatement. In January 1999 the Labour government recognised the unjustness of their treatment and agreed to pay the workers compensation for their unfair dismissal.

(186) In 1984 the National Association of Theatrical, Television and Kine Employees amalgamated with the Association of Broadcasting Staff to form the Broadcasting and Entertainment Trades Alliance.

(187) From 1989 to 1991 the Confederation of Shipbuilding and Engineering Unions ran a campaign to reduce the working week from thirty-nine to thirty-five hours. The campaign was only partly successful for ten years later the working week across most engineering industries is thirty-seven hours.

(188) Regrettably the GMB's jolly exhortation to its members to vote Labour at the 1992 General Election did not prevent the Tories under John Major from winning a fourth term in office.

(189) CLOSED BY THE TORIES is one of the most poignant illustrations of the Tory government's destruction of the coal mining industry between 1984 and 1994 – 185 pits closed and 18 privatised.

(190–193) With the amalgamation of the NALGO, NUPE and COHSE in 1993 the

resulting union, UNISON, became Britain's largest with over 1 million members drawn from every branch of the public services and some private industries. Three-quarters of its members are women although most of its senior officers are men. Using the cartoon figure of a bear, UNISON was the first trade union to run advertisements on television and was among several organisations whose advertising presented a more friendly image of trade unionism in the 1990s.

(194) In the aftermath of the First World War Britain established its own forests so as not be wholly dependant on timber imports. Over the next fifty years the Forestry Commission land was open to public access; then the Tories decided to sell off the Commission's land to private companies.

(195) In the face of a lack of democracy in the London-based TUC and its exclusion of trades councils seventy delegates from Scottish unions and trades councils met at the Berkeley Hall, Glasgow on 25–7 March 1897 and formed their own trades union congress.

(196) After a three-year pay freeze workers at Magnet Kitchens went on strike only to be sacked. After a twenty-month lockout a few of the original 320 workers voted to return to work in April 1998.

(197) Members of NUPE, NALGO and COHSE – amalgamated to make UNISON in 1993 – had formed the backbone of the National Health Service since it was established by a Labour government in 1948.

(198) The International Confederation of Free Trade unions was born in 1948 out of a refusal by the American Federation of Labour to accept the Russians into the World Federation of Trade Unions which had been constituted in Paris in October 1945.

(199) In July 1997 British Airways' cabin crews went on strike over an imposed cost-cutting and conditions package. As a result 70 per cent of flights out of Heathrow and Gatwick were grounded. When the employers threatened to declare the strike illegal hundreds of members of the TGWU and the British Airlines Stewards' and Stewardesses' Association phoned in to say that their absence was due to sickness.

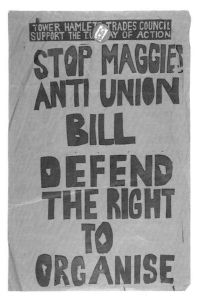

154. 1980. Tower Hamlets Trades Council.

155. 1980. National Union of Tailors and Garment Workers.

156. 1980. National Union of Tailors and Garment Workers.

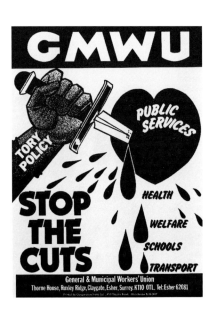

157. n.d. Northern Ireland Committee of the Irish Congress of Trade Unions.

158. n.d. Bakers, Food and Allied Workers' Union.

159. 1982. General and Municipal Workers' Union.

160. 1984. Greater London Council Staff Association.

161. 1982. Transport & General Workers' Union.

162. 1982. Trades Union Congress.

163. 1982. National Association of Local Government Workers/ National Union of Public Employees.

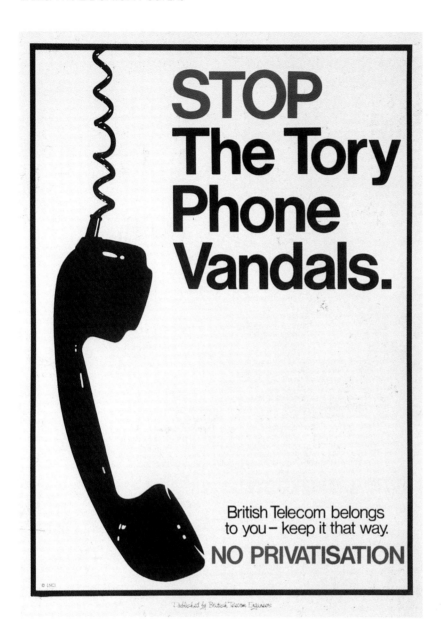

164. 1981. Union of Communication Workers.

165. 1984. National Association of Local Government Workers.

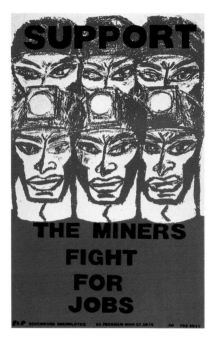

166–9. 1984. National Union of Mineworkers.

170. 1984. National Union of Journalists.

171. 1984. National Union of Mineworkers.

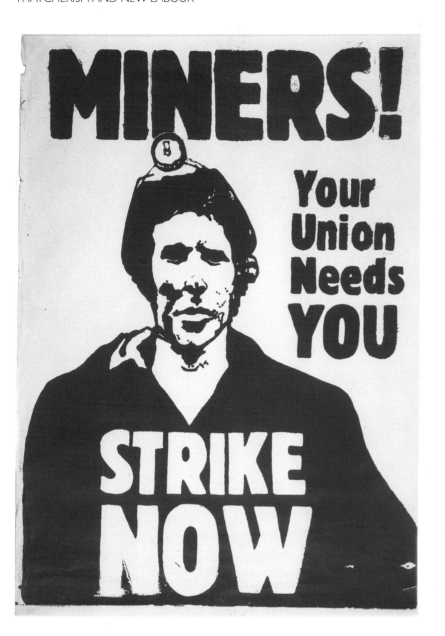

172. 1984. National Union of Mineworkers.

173. 1984. Women against Pit Closures/ National Union of Mineworkers.

IN THE
NATIONAL
INTEREST

Sat 24 Aug:
Snowdown Colliery (Aylesham New Club) 8pm

Wed 28 Aug-Sat 31 Aug:
PLEASANCE THEATRE (Venue 33) 10.30 am
EDINBURGH FESTIVAL FRINGE '85

Also at Monkton Hall and
Bilston Glen Collieries

PROCEEDS TO THE SACKED & IMPRISONED MINERS FUND

174. 1985. Mere Commodity Arts.

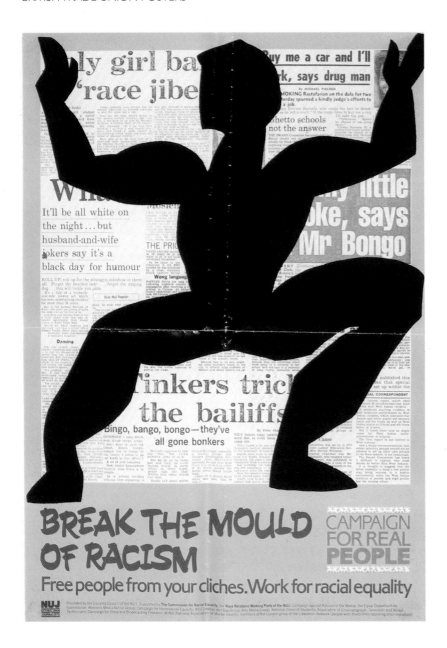

175. 1984. National Union of Journalists.

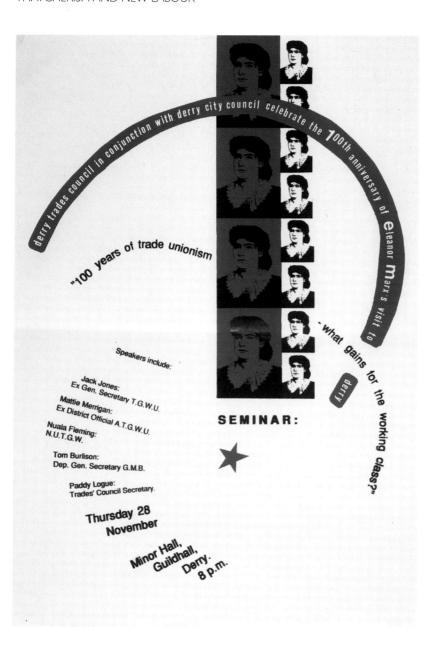

derry trades council in conjunction with derry city council celebrate the 100th anniversary of eleanor marx's visit to

"100 years of trade unionism

- what gains for the working class?"

derry

SEMINAR:

Speakers include:

Jack Jones:
Ex Gen. Secretary T.G.W.U.

Mattie Merrigan:
Ex District Official A.T.G.W.U.

Nuala Fleming:
N.U.T.G.W.

Tom Burlison:
Dep. Gen. Secretary G.M.B.

Paddy Logue:
Trades' Council Secretary.

Thursday 28
November

Minor Hall,
Guildhall,
Derry.
8 p.m.

176. 1985. Derry Trades Council.

177. 1986. NUPE members demonstrate against Tory government cuts in public services.

The truth?
He couldn't give
a XXXX

(If you care, don't buy Murdoch's papers: The Sun,
News of the World, Times & Sunday Times)

178. 1986. Society of Graphical and Allied Trades, National Graphical Association, Amalgamated
Union of Engineering Workers, National Union of Journalists.

179. 1988. National Association of Local Government Workers

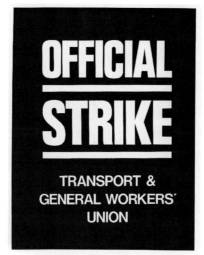

180. n.d. National Union of Journalists.
181. n.d. Transport & General Workers' Union.
182. n.d. National Association of Teachers in Further and Higher Education.
183. n.d. South-East Region of the Trades Union Congress.

184. 1988. Edinburgh Trades Council.

185. 1989. Trades Union Congress/Council of Civil Service Unions.

186. 1989. Broadcasting and Entertainment Trades Alliance.

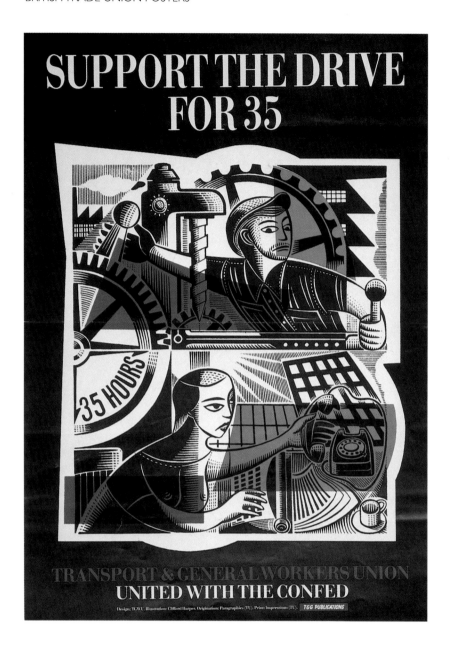

187. 1989. Transport & General Workers' Union.

188. 1992. General, Municipal, Boilermakers' Union.

189. 1995. The Savage Pen.

HE TORIES

Every effort has been made to get these details as accurate as possible. Closure dates may differ slightly depending on which part of the industry supplied them.

Where a Branch did not issue a Badge one has been chosen to represent them. Some Branches issued more than one Badge whilst other Badges were unobtainable.

Hopefully none of these selections will offend any present or ex-members but any slight inaccuracies cannot hide the fact that the Tories couldn't break the miners so they took away most of the industry and sold what was left, (exactly what they said they wouldn't do).

Letter sent to all miners in June 1984 from British Coal Chairman Ian MacGregor ,

"This is a strike which should never have happened. It is based on a very serious misrepresentation and distortion of the facts. At great financial cost, miners have supported the strike for 14 weeks because your leaders have told you this.... The Coal Board is out to butcher the industry. That we plan to do away with 70,000 jobs. That we plan to close down around 86 pits leaving only 100 working collieries.

If these things were true I would not blame miners for getting angry or for being deeply worried, but these things are absolutely untrue. I state that categorically and solemnly. You have been deliberately misled."

MacGregor was Knighted in 1986.

COAL, TIME THE AVENGER)

190. 1996. UNISON.

191. 1996. UNISON, Scotland Branch.

192. 1996. UNISON.

193. 1996. UNISON.

194. n.d. Transport & General Workers' Union.

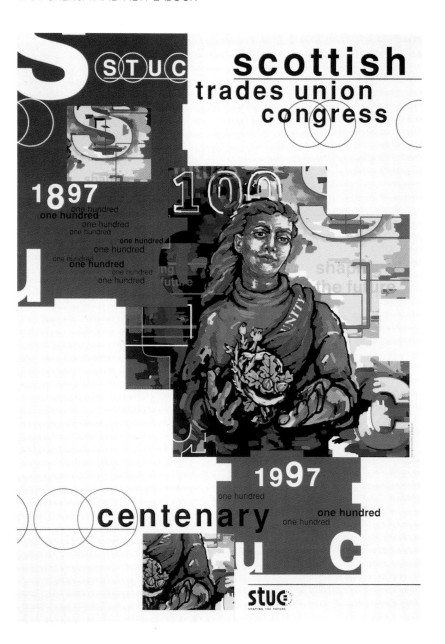

195. 1997. Scottish Trades Union Congress.

196. 1997. Magnet International Support Group.
197. 1998. UNISON

198. 1998. International Federation of Free Trade Unions.

199. 1998. Transport & General Workers' Union/ British Airlines Stewards and Stewardesses Association.

'We concede that labour may be regulated by the law of supply and demand. But is it? According to the law of supply and demand, "wages should have risen". There is more work — there would seem to be need of more work; more "demand", and proportionably less "supply", and yet our wages are the same at which they relatively stood. Oh! But says Messrs. Cash "I am a Capitalist — my capital employs your labour." Labour, independent labour first created capital, and plenty blessed the world! The capital being thus created, the question is — "shall it be absorbed by the few, or enjoyed by the many?" The Capitalist buys machinery. Where does he get the money? Out of his profits on the work of his men. The Capitalist pays wages. Where does he get the money? Out of his profits on the work of his men. The Capitalist lives in sumptuousness and splendour, and accumulates colossal fortunes. Where does he get the money? Out of his profits on the work of his men. Yes even the produce of wealth is one eternal system of creation; ever new — ever welling from its parent source — labour. Any and every moment the people draw from these clear fountains, close at their source — for they are themselves the source; — any moment they may drive avarice from troubling its stream.'

From a poster addressed 'To The Factory Operatives And Others' by the Coventry Ribbon Weavers' Association. 1856.

Sources

I am very grateful to the following organisations and individuals who have kindly given permission to reproduce their material in this book. I would also like to thank the librarians, curators and staff of the many libraries, archives and museums who gave of their time when this book was being researched.

John Gorman Collections: endpapers
Northumberland Record Office: 1, 13–16, 25–32, 34, 35
Morning Star: 2, 5 (Tony Benn), 7, 133, 177
Internationaal Instituut Voor Sociale Geschiedenis, Amsterdam: 3, 70
Hulton Getty: 4
National Museum of Labour History: 6, 51, 53, 55–6, 59, 64, 97–101, 104–23, 129, 132, 134–5, 148–150, 154–5, 168–73, 178, 189
British Library: 10–12, 23
Rochdale Libraries: 17, 19, 42
GMB/Peter Carter: 18, 62, 63, 72, 90, 91, 156, 158–61, 167, 176, 187–8
University of London Library: 20
Somerset Archive and Record Service: 21
Dorset Record Office: 22
James Klugmann Collection: 24
University of Warwick, Modern Records Centre: 33, 73
Coventry City Record Office: 36
Herbert Art Gallery, Coventry: 37
Trades Union Congress: 38, 52, 61, 66, 67, 74–89, 92–6, 131, 157, 162, 183, 174, 185
Buckinghamshire Record Office: 39
Tyne and Wear Archives Service: 40
British Library of Political and Economic Science: 41, 47, 58
Joe Flemming: 43
Wigan Archives Service: 44, 45
Essex Record Office: 46
Tower Hamlets Libraries: 49, 50
Ron Todd: 54

West Yorkshire Archive Service: 57
Manchester Police Museum: 60
Trades Union Congress: 61, 66, 102, 131
Norfolk Rural Life Museum: 65
Transport & General Workers' Union: 68, 126–8, 130, 136–7, 194 and 5 (Bill Morris) in the TGWU edition
Lichfield Joint Record Office: 69
University of Wales Swansea, South Wales Coalfield Collection: 71
Sid Brown: 124–5, 166, 180–2
Harold Smith: 138–40
Paul Martin: 140–4.
National Union of Teachers: 145
John Sturrock/Report: 146
Chippenham Posters: 147
UNISON: 151, 163, 165, 179, 190–3, 197
Andrew Wiard: 152 and 5 (Rodney Bickerstaffe) in the UNISON edition
Communication Workers' Union: 164
National Union of Journalists: 175
NATFHE: 177
Broadcasting, Entertainment, Cinematograph and Theatre Union: 186
Glasgow Caledonian University Library: 195
Framework: 196
Richard Ross: 198
The Guardian: 199

Much of the material used in preparing this book, together with many reproductions of posters not used, is now deposited at the National Museum of Labour History

SHOP
ASSISTANTS
STRIKE
SHOP
ASSISTANTS
STRIKE
SHOP
ASSISTANTS
SHOP
ASSISTANTS
STRIKE.